First World War
and Army of Occupation
War Diary
France, Belgium and Germany

24 DIVISION
Divisional Troops
Royal Army Veterinary Corps
36 Mobile Veterinary Section
1 September 1915 - 3 April 1919

WO95/2203/3

The Naval & Military Press Ltd
www.nmarchive.com
Published in association with The National Archives

Published by

The Naval & Military Press Ltd

Unit 10 Ridgewood Industrial Park,

Uckfield, East Sussex,

TN22 5QE England

Tel: +44 (0) 1825 749494

www.naval-military-press.com

www.nmarchive.com

This diary has been reprinted in facsimile from the original. Any imperfections are inevitably reproduced and the quality may fall short of modern type and cartographic standards.

© **Crown Copyright**
Images reproduced by permission of The National Archives, London, England, 2015.

Contents

Document type	Place/Title	Date From	Date To
Heading	WO95/2203/3		
Heading	36th Mobile Vety Section Sep 1915-Apr 1919		
Heading	24th Division 36th Mobile Vet. Sect. Vol I Sep 15		
War Diary	Deepcut	01/09/1915	01/09/1915
War Diary	Brookwood	01/09/1915	01/09/1915
War Diary	Southampton	01/09/1915	01/09/1915
War Diary	Havre	01/09/1915	02/09/1915
War Diary	Cinder City	03/09/1915	03/09/1915
War Diary	Havre Station	03/09/1915	03/09/1915
War Diary	Maresquel	03/09/1915	03/09/1915
War Diary	Neuville	04/09/1915	04/09/1915
War Diary	Beaurainville	06/09/1915	21/09/1915
War Diary	Laires	22/09/1915	23/09/1915
War Diary	Hanen.Artois	23/09/1915	24/09/1915
War Diary	Annezin	25/09/1915	25/09/1915
War Diary	Sailly Labourse	26/09/1915	29/09/1915
War Diary	St. Hilaire	30/09/1915	30/09/1915
Heading	24th Division 36th Mob. Vet. Sect. Vol: 2		
War Diary	St, Hilaire	01/10/1915	01/10/1915
War Diary	Aire	02/10/1915	02/10/1915
War Diary	Sercus	02/10/1915	03/10/1915
War Diary	Herzeele	03/10/1915	05/10/1915
War Diary	Godwaersvelde	06/10/1915	06/10/1915
War Diary	Westoutre	06/10/1915	31/10/1915
Heading	24th Division 36th Mob. Vet. Sect. Vol: 3 Nov 15		
War Diary	Westoutre	01/11/1915	24/11/1915
War Diary	Steenvorde	25/11/1915	26/11/1915
War Diary	Tilques	26/11/1915	30/11/1915
Heading	24th Div 36th Mob. Vet. Sect. Vol: 4		
War Diary	Tilques	01/12/1915	06/01/1916
War Diary	Noordpeene	07/01/1916	07/01/1916
War Diary	Steenvoorde Poperinghe	08/01/1916	08/01/1916
War Diary	Poperinghe	08/01/1916	31/01/1916
Heading	36th Map. Vet. Sect. Vol 6		
War Diary	Poperinghe	01/02/1916	29/02/1916
Heading	36 M Vets Vol 7		
War Diary	Poperinghe	01/03/1916	20/03/1916
War Diary	Fletre	21/03/1916	01/04/1916
War Diary	Nieppe	01/04/1916	05/07/1916
War Diary	Nr Bailleul	06/07/1916	09/07/1916
War Diary	Le. Seau.11th	11/07/1916	11/07/1916
War Diary	Le Seau Nr. Nieppe	11/07/1916	21/07/1916
War Diary	Coq De Paille	22/07/1916	25/07/1916
War Diary	Cavillon	26/07/1916	31/07/1916
War Diary	Corbie	01/08/1916	01/08/1916
War Diary	NaBray	02/08/1916	02/08/1916
War Diary	Bois de Tailles	03/08/1916	12/08/1916
War Diary	Meaulte	13/08/1916	06/09/1916
War Diary	Longpre	07/09/1916	07/09/1916
War Diary	Ailly. Le Haut Clocher	08/09/1916	16/09/1916

War Diary	Ailly	17/09/1916	18/09/1916
War Diary	Pontremy	19/09/1916	19/09/1916
War Diary	Pernes	20/09/1916	22/09/1916
War Diary	Bruay	23/09/1916	25/09/1916
War Diary	Fresnicourt	26/09/1916	28/10/1916
War Diary	Bruay	28/10/1916	28/10/1916
War Diary	Drouvin	30/10/1916	12/02/1917
War Diary	Ecquedecques	13/02/1917	05/03/1917
War Diary	Noeux Les Mines	06/03/1917	22/04/1917
War Diary	Fontes	23/04/1917	23/04/1917
War Diary	Matringhem	24/04/1917	08/05/1917
War Diary	Norrent Fontes	09/05/1917	09/05/1917
War Diary	Morbecque	10/05/1917	10/05/1917
War Diary	Steenvoorde	11/05/1917	12/05/1917
War Diary	Winnezeele	13/05/1917	15/05/1917
War Diary	Poperinghe	15/05/1917	27/05/1917
War Diary	Westoutre	28/05/1917	13/06/1917
War Diary	Nicholas	14/06/1917	20/06/1917
War Diary	Map 28 N1 Central	21/06/1917	30/06/1917
War Diary	N1 Central Forward Area	01/07/1917	03/07/1917
War Diary	Pradelles	04/07/1917	04/07/1917
War Diary	La. Belle Croix	05/07/1917	12/07/1917
War Diary	Pradelles	13/07/1917	14/07/1917
War Diary	M b Central Sheet 28	14/07/1917	22/07/1917
War Diary	M 6 b 3.3	23/07/1917	30/07/1917
War Diary	In The Field	01/08/1917	30/09/1917
Heading	War Diary of 36 Mobile Veterinary From October 1917		
War Diary	In The Field	01/10/1917	15/10/1917
War Diary	Field	16/10/1917	27/10/1917
War Diary	Vraignes	28/10/1917	31/10/1917
Heading	War Diary 36th Mobile Veterinary Section From Nov to Nov 30th 1917		
War Diary	Vraignes	02/11/1917	30/11/1917
Heading	36 Mobile Veterinary Section War Diary December 1917		
War Diary	Vraignes	01/12/1917	31/12/1917
Heading	36 Mobile Veterinary Section War Diary for the month of January 1918		
War Diary	Vraignes	01/01/1918	31/01/1918
Heading	36 Mobile Veterinary Section War Diary for the month of February 1918		
War Diary	Vraignes	01/02/1918	28/02/1918
Heading	36 Mobile Veterinary Section 24 Division War Diary for the month of March 1918		
War Diary	Vraignes	01/03/1918	03/03/1918
War Diary	Bouvincourt	04/03/1918	13/03/1918
War Diary	Tertry	14/03/1918	24/03/1918
War Diary	Harbonnieres	25/03/1918	26/03/1918
War Diary	Tainnes	27/03/1918	28/03/1918
War Diary	Cottenchy	29/03/1918	30/03/1918
War Diary	Buyon	31/03/1918	31/03/1918
Heading	32 War Diary for the month of April 1918 36 Mobile Veterinary Section.		
War Diary	Buyon	01/04/1918	04/04/1918
War Diary	Vers	05/04/1918	06/04/1918
War Diary	Petit Cagny	07/04/1918	07/04/1918

War Diary	Clairy	08/04/1918	09/04/1918
War Diary	Andainville	10/04/1918	11/04/1918
War Diary	Wanel	12/04/1918	17/04/1918
War Diary	Buigny L'abbe	18/04/1918	18/04/1918
War Diary	Beauvis Wavens	19/04/1918	19/04/1918
War Diary	Ramecourt	20/04/1918	21/04/1918
War Diary	Le Cauroy	22/04/1918	30/04/1918
Heading	36 Mobile Veterinary Section War Diary May 1918		
War Diary		01/05/1918	16/05/1918
War Diary	In The Field	17/05/1918	31/05/1918
Heading	War Diary 36 Mobile Veterinary Section for the month of June 1918		
War Diary	Fosse 10	01/06/1918	30/06/1918
Heading	War Diary 36 Mobile Veterinary Section for the month of July 1918		
War Diary	Fosse 10	01/07/1918	31/07/1918
Heading	War Diary 36 Mobile Veterinary Section for the month of August 1918		
War Diary	Fosse 10	01/08/1918	16/08/1918
War Diary	Bouvigny Boyeffles	17/08/1918	31/08/1918
Heading	War Diary 36 Mobile Veterinary Section for the month of September 1918		
War Diary	Bouvigny	01/09/1918	30/09/1918
Heading	War Diary 36 Mobile Veterinary Section for the month of October 1918		
War Diary	La Folie Farm Lucheux	01/10/1918	05/10/1918
War Diary	Mercatel	06/10/1918	06/10/1918
War Diary	Moeuvres	07/10/1918	09/10/1918
War Diary	Graincourt	10/10/1918	10/10/1918
War Diary	Caurior	11/10/1918	13/10/1918
War Diary	Avesnes-Les-Aubert	14/10/1918	18/10/1918
War Diary	Cambrai	19/10/1918	26/10/1918
War Diary	St. Aubert	27/10/1918	30/11/1918
Miscellaneous Heading	On His Majesty's Service.		
War Diary	Landas	19/12/1918	19/12/1918
War Diary	Tournai	24/12/1918	27/12/1918
War Diary	La Tombe	24/01/1919	19/02/1919
War Diary	Tournai	24/02/1919	03/04/1919

WO95/32013

24TH DIVISION
DIVL TROOPS

36TH MOBILE VETY SECTION
SEP 1915 - APR 1919

24TH DIVISION
DIVL TROOPS

121/7153

24th Division

36th Mobile Vet: Sech:

Vol I

Sept. 15 — Apr. 19

Army Form C. 2118

WAR DIARY or INTELLIGENCE SUMMARY
(Erase heading not required.)

Instructions regarding War Diaries and Intelligence Summaries are contained in F.S. Regs., Part II. and the Staff Manual respectively. Title Pages will be prepared in manuscript.

36th MOBILE VETERINARY SECTION
Date Sept 1915

Place	Date	Hour	Summary of Events and Information	Remarks and references to Appendices
DEEPCUT	Sept 1	10 AM	The 36th Mobile Vety Sec left Deepcut fully equipped including 26 horses 3 waggons 1 Officer & 27 other ranks marched to Brookwood & arrived at 11 a.m. entrained uneventfully in the rain	
BROOKWOOD	"	11 AM		
"	1	1 PM	left at 1 PM. an uneventful journey to Southampton which was reached with lots of time to spare	
SOUTHAMPTON	1	3 PM	in good time at 3 PM ran alongside ship & entrained in S.S. Maidan all safely on board	
HAVRE	1	5.30 PM	embarked at 5.30. arrived at Havre after a wet but quiet trip. Lay to till 7 a.m. & disembarked	
"	2nd	7 AM	horses waggons & men. marched to Cinder City camp and stayed there till midnight.	
CINDER CITY	3rd	12.30 AM	Here Pte Brockwell was unwell sent to Hospital & detained. Left at 12.30 AM a dreadful night of thunder	
HAVRE-STATION	3rd	5.15 AM	Rain & lightning, arrived at Station 1.50 AM entrained with ocean of time & left at 5.15 AM. Had an uneventful	
MARESQUEL	3rd	7.30 PM	journey all day long and constant rain & arrived at 7.30 PM Maresquel Station. Jackies very few for	
"		10.30 PM	disembarking especially waggons, had to ride them dismantling in darkness & rain. Started off at 10.30 PM	
NEUVILLE	4th	2.30 AM	& marched 12½ miles arrived at Neuville 2.30 a.m., no billeting arrangements made. Billets had especially	
"		10.15 AM	Officers eventually got into a farm yard. Stayed here till Sunday & then moved to Beaurainville	
BEAURAINVILLE	6th	12.30	leaving Neuville 10.15 arriving Beaurainville 12.30 PM. Billeting had here also. nothing done for	
"			Officers especially.	
"			Horses unfit for service arrive daily are dressed & cared for & eventually sent per rail to Hospital	
"	9.12th	6 AM	16 lame horses & mules entrained at Beaurainville in transit for Abbeville in charge of 1 C.N.C.O. & 2 men.	
"			The train arrived the same night. But the party had to wait for veterinary dungs till the next day	
"			& by some mischance were sent to Boulogne & did not get back here till Wed Sept 15th.	
"	9.17th	6.30 PM	Received instructions from HqtrsD.A. as follows Supplies for 19th will be refilled on the Beaurainville	
"			Maresquel Rd 8 PM to night for information & compliance. This was complied with units appear to have been	
"			in the alert all night but nothing definite transpired. Sent off further batch of 16 injured animals	
"	9.18th		to Abbeville Vety Hospital. Usual daily routine of attention to sick animals	

WAR DIARY or INTELLIGENCE SUMMARY

Army Form C.2118

36th MOBILE VETERINARY SECTION
Date 19 Sept 15

Place	Date	Hour	Summary of Events and Information	Remarks and references to Appendices
BEAURAINVILLE	SEP 19		Usual morning routine. 5 cases still in Hospital, visited by A.D.V.S	
"	20		8 P.M. Visit from A.D.V.S with orders for sending away horses & warned us to be ready to move off at moment's notice	
"	21		12 Horses sent away to Abbeville with NCO & 2 men, had busy time collecting sick horses, and received orders to move off at 7 a.m. the next day.	
LAIRES	22		5:30 Reveille everything in good order with waggons packed, section moved off complete at 7.15 a.m. made good progress to Roye. Although troubled by the very inferior horses supplied by the divisional train to the supply waggon attached to us. collected sick mule at Roye. for which receipt was given, Picked up en route an injured man of the Middlesex Regt. The two horses of the supply waggon, attached to us from the supply train, were totally inadequate for the work & delayed us several hours. We had ended to use our own horses. We proceeded to Fruges where we encamped for two hours, moved off again at 3 P.M. passing through LUGY. HEZECQUES. BEAUMETZ-LES-AIRE. and on to LAIRES where we arrived at 6 P.M. finding it full of infantry. We found billets, at 4 P.M. the infantry moved off, and I enquired of all units if any of them had left sick horses or mules behind and was answered in the negative. A fine night and we had heavy gunfire all night	
LAIRES	23		Left Laires in good order at 7 a.m and made good progress through Febvin Palfart	

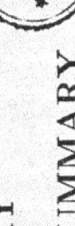

WAR DIARY or INTELLIGENCE SUMMARY

Army Form C.2118

35th MOBILE VETERINARY SECTION
Date 23.9.15

Place	Date	Hour	Summary of Events and Information	Remarks and references to Appendices
HAN-EN-ARTOIS	SEP 23		WESTREHAM, ST.HILAIRE. reaching HAM-EN-ARTOIS. about 11 A.M. from billet as usual	
	24		Collected 1 horse & 1 mule from MOLLINGHAM under Col Newsomes orders shot & buried 1 mule & 1 horse left at 7.45 P.M. in the dark & went right through to ANNEZIN arriving there 11 P.M. found a miserable billet & settled down for the night	
ANNEZIN	25		Nothing of interest except evacuation of 8 sick horses to ABBEVILLE	
			At three P.M received orders from A.D.V.S. to move at once and were on the move, we arrived at	
SAILLY-LABOURSE	26		SAILLY-LABOURSE. 6.30 but were delayed in the town by infantry and finally got into our billeting field 8 P.M	
	27		No special events as far as the section was concerned. but troops were constantly passing through to the trenches & wounded returning gun firing being very heavy.	
	28		Evacuated 13 horses from our section & 3 from the 12th Mobile Section to make 16. to ABBEVILLE. Orders to move being imminent we transferred 6 sick horses that had just come in to the 12th Mobile.	
	29		Left SAILLY-LABOURSE at 8 under shocking weather conditions which prevailed all day. held up on the march for 2 hours by incoming infantry, we proceeded to LILLERS. where we had an hours halt, then continued our march reaching ST HILAIRE 2.30 P.M.	
ST.HILAIRE	30		Checked stores & gear as we expected to stay here a few days. All through the month both men & horses have been well fed. rations never being short, men & horses all in good condition. during the month 90 horses have been taken in by the section. 66 Evacuated to Hospital 11 returned to units. 6 destroyed. 5 transferred to 12 Mobile Section 2 remaining with section	

W. Barron
Capt. A.V.C.

121/7608

24th Division

36th Mob. Vet. Sect.
Vol. 2

Oct 15

WAR DIARY
or
INTELLIGENCE SUMMARY

(Erase heading not required.)

Army Form C. 2118

Instructions regarding War Diaries and Intelligence Summaries are contained in F.S. Regs., Part II. and the Staff Manual respectively. Title Pages will be prepared in manuscript.

36th MOBILE VETERINARY SECTION
Date 1·10·15

Place	Date	Hour	Summary of Events and Information	Remarks and references to Appendices
ST.HILAIRE.	Oct 1		at ST.HILAIRE evacuated 14 horses to NEUFCHATEL	
AIRE	Oct 2		Left ST.HILAIRE. 11.30 AM. stopped at AIRE.STATION evacuated 10 sick horses for NEUFCHATEL. had lunch then proceeded	
SERCUS	Oct 2		on way to CERCUS arriving there 4.30 PM stopped night there	
	Oct 3		Left CERCUS at 8.30 a.m. En route shot a mule. Passed through CASSEL. STEENVORDE. WINNEZEELE. sent on in advance billeting party to HERZEELE. could get no satisfaction from anyone, eventually had to encamp on piece of waste ground.	
HERZEELE	Oct 3			
"	Oct 4		in town. managed to pass the night miserably here. Found an excellent billet next day. It appears to me to be a far better idea for the Mobile Vety Section to have a billet far out of the town, so that it can get a billet suited to its requirements after divisions left for new billet 1 KIL from HERZEELE kept very busy here with sick & wounded horses	
"	Oct 5		Vicinity from the ADVS & DDVS.	
GODVAERSVELDE	Oct 6		Left Herzeele at 10 A.M. with 70 horses arrived at GOEDVAERSVELDE. STATION 12.30 were kept waiting there till 4 PM & finally evacuated 36 horses at 4.30. uneventful journey to Westoutre. where we finally arrived at our new billet in the dark. Bad road the last ½ mile in wet clay road. and water supply for horses about 1 mile away from billet	
WESTOUTRE				
"	Oct 7		Considerable difficulty in finding refilling point for rations & forage. putting up lines for sick horses	
"	Oct 8		Rode down to RENINGHELST to see ADVS	
"	Oct 9		Got mackintoshes for whole section from DADOS. men working making winter stabling	
	Oct 10		Men busy working away at drains & winter stabling	
	Oct 11		Evacuated 24 horses to NEUFCHATEL from GODVAERSVELDE.STATION	

WAR DIARY
or
INTELLIGENCE SUMMARY
(Erase heading not required.)

Army Form C. 2118

Instructions regarding War Diaries and Intelligence Summaries are contained in F.S. Regs, Part II. and the Staff Manual respectively. Title Pages will be prepared in manuscript.

Place	Date	Hour	Summary of Events and Information	Remarks and references to Appendices
WESTOUTRE	Oct 12		Men busy erecting winter stables	
"	Oct 13		Capt Barrow left in morn in ambulance owing to attack of shingles & nerve trouble. A.D.V.S. called & made temporary arrangements re work during temporary absence of C.O. Sergt Massey & 91 men collected from horses from HARINGHE.	
"	Oct 14		Lt Dobie called & signed papers in aft. morn. Sergt Massey collected 1 horse HARINGHE men clearing out barns & sheds for stables	
"	Oct 15		Sergeant Crisp went down to see Ongar leaving A.D.V.S. & to Ordnance re clothing, boots, served out boots etc to men	
"	Oct 16		A.D.V.S. called in morn. Men busy making winter stables Captain Coulombe C.A.V.C. arrived in aft. took over command of 36 Mob Vety Section, groom also arrived.	
"	Oct 17		A.D.V.S. I called in morn re pay of men. Capt Coulombe paid men in aft.	
"	Oct 18		A.D.V.S. I called in morn re horses to GODVAERSVELDE. Capt Coulombe went with when 44 horses for NEUFCHATEL. SERGEANT. APPLEBY A.V.C arrived in aft under orders from Base Horse Depot annual reported to A.D.V.S. 14 sick horses & 3 cwt NCOs & 2 men I/C conducting party for NEUFCHATEL.	
"	Oct 19		Usual routine of Hospital work.	
"	Oct 20		Several horses from Ralph's H.P.A. Came for teeth attention etc Lt Dobie called for drugs in aft. usual routine work.	
"	Oct 21		Visit from the ADVS in morn & Chief Inspector, referring to Billeting amounts. Busy with weekly return in aft.	
"	Oct 22		Capt Coulombe went with ADVS to collect site for advance collecting station H.31. D.5. Map no 28 Ypres site selected	
"	Oct 23		Upon men putting up new & strengthening old horse lines	
"	Oct 24		Visit from A.D.V.S. in morn. usual routine of hospital work. Usual routine of hospital work.	

WAR DIARY
or
INTELLIGENCE SUMMARY
(Erase heading not required.)

Army Form C. 2118

36th MOBILE VETERINARY SECTION
Date 25/10/15

Place	Date	Hour	Summary of Events and Information	Remarks and references to Appendices
WESTOUTRE	Oct 25		Rain hard all day. 73 Inf Bgde called for horse ambulance helmets. 108 Bde R.F.A. & 104 Bde R.F.A. all supplied with same. A.D.V.S. called reference evacuating sick horses for to-morrow (26th) 1 horse destroyed philipoy	
"	Oct 26		Mule destroyed (fractured femur) Visit from the A.D.V.S. 16 horses evacuated to Neufchatel with C.B.O. & 1 man in morning. Rain all day.	
"	Oct 27		L/Cpl Benton representing 36 Mob. Vety. Section. attended Ceremonial Parade In RENINGHELST. Men dig -ging hole & burying horse in morn, rain most of day.	
"	Oct 28		rain all day. C.B.O. & 1 man returned from Neufchatel in morn. visit from A.D.V.S. 3 loads of rubble came for stable lines in aft. 1 Bay mare Draught (sick) from 10 Bde R.G.A. came in. float for treatment. Captain Coulombe went down to the A.D.V.S. in morn. men in aft getting ground ready for winter stabling	
"	Oct 29			
"	Oct 30		Visit from A.D.V.S. in morn. men putting down broken bricks for standings in stables.	
"	Oct 31		Capt Coulombe went down to Hull Section re mens pay. crushin not arriv. went in to R.E. re timber for winter stabling. Message from A.D.V.S. re appointment of Lieut Lawrie A.V.C. to take over 36 Mobile Vety. Section	

Henri E. Coulombe Capt. C.A.V.C.
Temp. O.C. 36 Mobile Vety Section

36t. hdb: Vet: Seek.
Vol: 3

12/7693

34th Braun

Nov 15

aus

WAR DIARY or INTELLIGENCE SUMMARY

Army Form C. 2118

Place	Date	Hour	Summary of Events and Information	Remarks and references to Appendices
WESTOUTRE	Nov 1.		Rain all day. A.D.V.S. called in morn re shortly evacuating	
"	2		Rain all day. Corpl Benton & limber waggon. carted away Capt Borlunbis kit to the Canadian Division. Capt Borlunbe left the section in aft. Lieut Laurie arrived & took over command of Section	
"	3		16 Horses evacuated to Sherfsdale Veterinary Hospital in morn Lieut Laurie went with party to Goodswerrelds, C.V.C.O. & I man went with horses by train. Rain at intervals during day. A.D.V.S. arrived in aft. Lieut Laurie paid men in aft.	
"	4		Rain part of day. horse died of debility. men bringing some. 2 French speaking privates went round different farms re remount purchasing trials for winter stabling in aft. It apparently put on strength	
"	5		Lieut Laurie went down to A.D.V.S. with weekly return. orderly went to Poperinghe re fence, timber for stabling. Corpl Benton & pte Shearer returned from Shersdale Vety Hospital aft taking sick horses away from section.	
"	6		A.D.V.S. called in morning re fence. halter. 2 thing Corpl Benton back in car with halters. Lieut Laurie went to RENINGHELST re timber for stabling. Pte Beaumont under instructions from A.D.V.S. altering horse rugs. Corpl Joplin & waggon with men brought timber for stabling from Poperinghe	
"	7		Visit from A.D.V.S. re fence evacuating on 8th inst.	
"	8		Belgian Carpenters & our own & one man from section starting framework for winter stables Corporal Joplin & 4 men went away with 34 (34) sick horses to NEUCHATEL vety hospital. 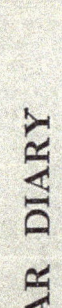 Pte Newman went down to WESTOURTRE re billeting certificate. Capt Blackburn A.V.S. called in aft.	

Army Form C. 21[?].

WAR DIARY
or
INTELLIGENCE SUMMARY.

(Erase heading not required.)

Instructions regarding War Diaries and Intelligence Summaries are contained in F. S. Regs., Part II. and the Staff Manual respectively. Title pages will be prepared in manuscript.

26th MOBILE
Date 9/11/15
VETERINARY SECTION

Place	Date	Hour	Summary of Events and Information	Remarks and references to Appendices
	Nov			
WESTOUTRE	9		Rain part of day. all afn men & Belgians busy at winter stable erections for horses, freeing up framework. Visit from A.D.V.S in morn	
"	10		Drizzled entirely rode to BAILLEUL for mails in morn. Belgians (2) & spare men of section busy erecting stables. A.D.V.S called in aft. men with waggon getting straw & sand. Flurry went all day. hailstorm in aft	
"	11		2 Belgians & men from section busy all day erecting stables - straw & sand brought for same in waggons. Visit from A.D.V.S in aft	
"	12		C.E. went to RENINGHELST in morn & to POPERINGHE in aft, rain all day.	
"	13		Strong gale & rain all day. men with C.E. strengthening building against [?] 2 Belgians came in aft & put thatch on stable roof. A.D.V.S. called in aft.	
"	14		Fine day, Belgians at work thatching roof of stable, men getting straw & sand for same. Visit from A.D.V.S in aft.	
"	15		Fine day, Belgians finished thatching in morn. Levelling ground ready for building floor. C.E. went to R.E. reference timber & cement used in building	
"	16		Orderly went to GOUDVAERSVELDE in morn & ordered trucks for sick Horses. 14 sick Horses went to NEUFCHATEL with Conpl Berlin. Pte Prior & Greener O.C & A.D.V.S went with party to GOUDVAERSVELDE STATION.	

WAR DIARY
or
INTELLIGENCE SUMMARY.
(Erase heading not required.)

Army Form C. 2118.

Place	Date	Hour	Summary of Events and Information	Remarks and references to Appendices
	NOV			
WESTOUTRE	17		Rain & hailstorms men levelling floor of stable. G.S. Limbers went to Ordnance Stores & R.E. men o/ft. for timber, canvas, & blankets for men.	
"	18		Visit from A.D.V.S. in morn, heavy frost in morn, rain in aft. men working at new stable floor. Corpl Benton Pte Gunn & Prior returned from NEUFCHATEL in evening	
"	19		C.C. went down to A.D.V.S. in morn. Heavy frost in morn. Visit from A.D.V.S. in aft re evacuating. Large number of horses (15) received for treatment from various units	
"	20		Fine day. A.D.V.S. called in morn, several horses in for treatment. Sergt Massey went to GOUDVAERSVELDE re ordering trucks for evacuating. C'l Benton went to Ordnance at REN-INGHELST. 2 horses destroyed	
"	21		Men from sickness went to GOUDVAERSVELDE STATION with 50 horses (including 5 mange cases) in aft. Pte Leifer Beaumont, & Uplin went with same to NEUCHATEL Vety Hospital. CORPL Taflin. Pte Leifer Beaumont, & Uplin went with same to NEUCHATEL Vety Hospital ADVS called in aft. ADVS + OC Probit 3rd Division called in aft.	
"	22		2 horses destroyed. Fine day, heavy frost in morn. cleaning up camp preparatory to moving	
"	23		Fine day. men clearing up camp etc. preparatory to leaving, rifles etc. return of Corpl Taflin Ptes Leifer Beaumont & Uplin from NEUFCHATEL Vety Hospital	

WAR DIARY or INTELLIGENCE SUMMARY

Army Form C. 2118.

36th MOBILE VETERINARY SECTION Date 24.11.15

Place	Date Nov.	Hour	Summary of Events and Information	Remarks and references to Appendices
WESTOUTRE	24		O.C. went to RENINGHELST. for hay & section. Corpl Benton & Pte Hall went to NEUFCHATEL with 11 sick horses for Vety Hospital. O.C. went with Sergt Appleby & men to GOUDVAERSVELDE STATION with horses for above. Men packing up waggons & tidying up preparatory to leaving on 25th. Men paid in aft.	
"	"			
"	"			
STEENVORDE	25		Section left 9.45 AM. uneventful journey arrived at billet 3.0 clock PM. Sergt Appleby & Pte Hunn went on ahead to collect 2 horses at HERZEELE. FINE DAY.	
"	26		Section left Billet near STEENVOORDE in morn 8.30. FINE DAY.	
TILQUES	26		STEENVOORDE in morn 8.30. for TILQUES VIA HAZEBROUCK. WALLON-CAPPEL. EBBLINGHEM. ARQUES. ST OMER arrived at billet 5 PM. transport wagon arrived 6.30 PM. Some hailstorms en route. uneventful journey & everything arrived in good order & condition	
"	27		Section all busy fixing up quarters, putting up horse lines for sick animals, fine day, heavy frost in morn.	
"	28		9 men & 1 N.C.O went Church parade. O.C. took Section out exercise (mounted). O.C. went to MOULLE - destroyed horse left by 64 Bty R.F.A. Frost in morn, fine day.	
"	29		Visit from the D.D.V.S in morn. Vet inspection in aft. rain in morning Visit from A.D.V.S in morn. D.D.V.S inspected Section everything satisfactory except	

Army Form C. 2118.

WAR DIARY
or
INTELLIGENCE SUMMARY
(Erase heading not required.)

Instructions regarding War Diaries and Intelligence Summaries are contained in F. S. Regs., Part II and the Staff Manual respectively. Title pages will be prepared in manuscript.

[Stamp: 36th MOBILE VETERINARY SECTION Date 30 NOV]

Places	Date	Hour	Summary of Events and Information	Remarks and references to Appendices
TILQUES	NOV 29		description of horses sent to Base Hospital, which was not complete enough in details. Visit from A.D.V.S. in morn. acting Sergt "many" evacuated to field ambulance 73rd	
	30		wet day.	

J. R. Karr
Lieut. A.V.C.
O.C. 36 Mobile Vety Section.

36th Inf: Vet: Sect:
Vol: 4

1/
798

WAR DIARY
or
INTELLIGENCE SUMMARY.
(Erase heading not required.)

Army Form C. 2118.

36th MOBILE VETERINARY SECTION
Date 1.12.15

Place	Date	Hour	Summary of Events and Information	Remarks and references to Appendices
TILQUES	DEC 1		Rain & wind all day. 31 sick horses arrived, preparing evacuation lists etc. A.D.V.S called in morn. Double piquet at night on account of large number of horses. 1 horse returned to unit	
	2		Corpl Yoplin Pte Leifer Greener & Miller went away with 33 sick horses to NEUFCHATEL. No 13 VETY. HOSPITAL. O.C. rode down with horses & return to WATTEN STATION & saw horses entrained for same (Aseveral horses arrived from different units during day. Rain & wind all day. Dinner	
	3		O.C. went to A.D.V.S. with weekly returns, & visited Glasgow Yeomanry in aft (inspection) rain all day. 8 horses arrived from various units during day. Visit from A.D.V.S. in morn.	
	4		Wind & rainy. 1 horse received for treatment. Visit from A.D.V.S. C.E. went round Sherwood Foresters & Glasgow Yeomanry in aft.	
	5		Return of Cpl Yoplin Pte Miller Greener & Leifer from NEUFCHATEL in morn. 1st C.R.I.S.P. left for ENGLAND on leave. Visit from A.D.V.S. dull day, no rain during day.	
	6		Wind & rain 5 horses evited for treatment. Orderly rode down to WATTEN re ordering trucks. A.D.V.S. called in evening.	
	7		Corpl Berlin Pte Beaumont Upton Wright went to NEUFCHATEL VETY. HOSPITAL NO 13	

1577 Wt. W10791/1773 500,000 1/15 D. D. & L. A.D.S.S./Forms/C. 2118.

WAR DIARY
or
INTELLIGENCE SUMMARY.
(Erase heading not required.)

Army Form C. 2118.

Place	Date	Hour	Summary of Events and Information	Remarks and references to Appendices
	DEC			
TILQUES	7 cont'd		with 30 sick horses. C.E. went down in with section & entrained same at WATTEN.	
"	8		windy dull day. A.D.V.S. (locum tenens) to work of A.D.V.S. (to transact business) 3 sick horses entered for treatment	
			C.E. went in morning to ADVS. (to transact business) 12 sick horses entered for treatment	
			windy dull day. C.E. & Pte D. infected Plenwood Yorkshire. 3 cast horses entered for base (cast by D.D.R)	
"	9		C.E. & men took 16 horses down to WATTEN entrained same for NO.13. VETY.HOSPITAL. NEUFCHATEL	
			Corpl Yafflin Ptes Trivetts Hutchinson went with horses. rain. C.E. went to ADVS office (in place	
			of ADVS. on leave) received 4 horses for treatment	
"	10		Rainy day. C.E. went to ADVS office in morn 5 horses received for treatment	
			Corpl Benton. Pte Beaumont. r.w.right. returned from evacuating in morn.	
"	11.		Rainy Day Cpl Benton & Limber G.S. wagon went to WATTEN. STAT." for kidstalls	
			C.S. Pte Quilter Gunn. Greener. & Upton. went to ARNEKE. NORDPEENE. OCHTEZEELE. & collected	
			5 horses Lt Leask AVC. called in morn C.E. went round to ADVS (to transact business) 6 horses	
			entered for treatment	
"	12.		rain in morn Pte Prior & Dr Impey went with float for sick horse in aft.	
			Cpl Yafflin Pte Trivetts & Hutchinson returned from evacuating horses. Lt Cripp returned from leave.	

WAR DIARY
or
INTELLIGENCE SUMMARY.
(Erase heading not required.)

Army Form C. 2118.

Place	Date	Hour	Summary of Events and Information	Remarks and references to Appendices
TILQUES	DEC 12 contd		4 horses received for treatment. C.L. went to ADVS. office (to sign hyper etc)	
	13		Fine day. 15 horses received for treatment etc. C.L. went to inspect various units in absence of ADVS. (R.E. Field Ab. L.C.E. & Signal Co.)	
	14		34 horses evacuated to No. 13 Vety. Hospital. Neufchatel. Corpl Benton, Pte Green, Hall, Prior & Shannon went with horses. C.L. went to St Martins on business. ADVS.	
	15		Fine day. 3 horses received for treatment. Windy. 6 horses received for treatment. A.D.V.S. visited us in morn. Drove Hulluken T.35609 evacuated to No 20 C.C. Station in morning.	
	16		Fine day. horses entered for treatment	
	17		Return of Cpl Benton, Pte Green, Shannon, Prior & Hall. from Evacuating horses at NEUFCHATEL. 10 horses entered for treatment. rainy day.	
	18		Dull misty day. 16 horses entered for treatment. visit from ADVS. in aft. 1 horse destroyed	
	19		Fine day. 11 horses entered for treatment. visit from ADVS. Making up of evacuating rolls in aft. Corpl Joplin, Pte Miller, Hallett & Birr went with horses to NEUFCHATEL. C.L. Sergt Appleby went with horses to WATTEN STATION to entrain. 1 horse destroyed in morn, 11 horses entered for treatment. Fine day. Visit from ADVS in aft. Sgt Briop 3215 Evacuated to St Omer Casualty Clearing Station	
	20			

WAR DIARY
or
INTELLIGENCE SUMMARY.
(Erase heading not required.)

Army Form C. 2118.

Place	Date	Hour	Summary of Events and Information	Remarks and references to Appendices
TILQUES	DEC 21st		Rainy day. C.O. rode to Tatinghem re baggage waggon. 7 horses entered for treatment return of Corpl Taplin, Pte Mullin, Pte. Hallett from evacuating horses at NEUFCHATEL. Rainy day. 1 horses received for treatment. C.O. visited Sherwood Foresters	
	22		in aft & inspected horses	
	23		Horses received for treatment. Wet day. Visit from A.D.V.S. 1 horse destroyed	
	24		Wet Day. 4 Horses received for treatment. A.D.V.S. called in morn. Sick horses put in new paddock on account of mud.	
	25		Rain in morn. 17 horses received for treatment. Visit from ADVS in morn.	
	26		107 Horses evacuated to NEUFCHATEL. VETY. HOSPITAL. in morn O.E. Seaforth green of section (about 10 men of GLASGOW YEOMANRY arriving with horses to relieve) Corpl Nunn 1/c & 6 men taking horses to NEUFCHATEL. Visit from ADVS in aft. 2 horses received for treatment—	
	27		34 Evacuated from 24th Division, 73 evacuated from other formations. Fine day. C.O. went in morn & inspected horses of Sherwood Foresters. Windy day with rain, no horses received for treatment	
	28		Fine day. 7 horses entered for treatment, visit from A.D.V.S. in aft. return of Corpl Nunn & 6 men from NEUFCHATEL. VETY. HOSPITAL. Corpl TAPLIN thrown from his horse	

WAR DIARY
or
INTELLIGENCE SUMMARY.
(Erase heading not required.)

Army Form C. 2118.

36th MOBILE
Date 28.12.15
VETERINARY SECTION

Place	Date	Hour	Summary of Events and Information	Remarks and references to Appendices
TILQUES	Dec contd 28		On returning from Refilling point, picked up unconscious & taken to Hospital No 20 CCS ST OMER.	
"	29		Pte. HALL 5104 evacuated to Field Ambulance ← to 20 CCS on account of eyes. fine day, 19 horses received for treatment. Visit from the DDVS & ADVS in afl.	
"	30		Driver Hutchinson. J 35609. evacuated to No 20 CCS. this day returned to duty, 6 horses received for treatment. fine day.	
"	31		Sergt Benton Pte Ayers & Prior went with horses 32 to NEUFCHATEL VETY. HOSPITAL 6 lame men of section continued some at WATTEN in morn. 20 horses received for treatment. rainy day. Received horse from 1st W Lancs Bde RFA destroyed immediately on arrival at section some units apparently consider horse & vety feeding merely a fatigue party to bury dead animals.	

J F Laurie Lieut A.V.C
O.C 36 Mobile Vety Section.

WAR DIARY or INTELLIGENCE SUMMARY

Army Form C. 2118.

Place	Date	Hour	Summary of Events and Information	Remarks and references to Appendices
TILQUES	JAN 1st		Windy day with rain. 16 horses received for treatment. 1 horse destroyed. 4 went Lanes B-de. Horse inspected if fetlock joint OH	
"	2		Windy day with rain. 3 horses received for treatment. 2 horses destroyed. (1) 24 D.A.C. (2) 4 went Lanes Bde. A.S.V.S culled in aft. Corpl TAPLIN returned to duty from Hospital ST OMER	
"	3		Windy day 15 horses received for treatment. DDVS inspected horses (mange cases) in aft.	
"	4		Windy day with rain. 46 horses evacuated to ST OMER STATION for NEUFCHATEL VETY HOSPITAL in morn. CL went down to see entraining. Corpl Mann Pte Bros & Hewitt conducting party.	
"	5		Horses received for treatment. 2 horses destroyed in morn. ABT 52 Brigade. C.L. Pte Gregson & Green collected horses (from) CLERQUES. C.L went to BONNINGHEM in aft. 4 horses received for treatment. Men all busy packing up preparatory to leaving on 6th	
"	6		Section left TILQUES in morn for NOORDPEENE 9.45 am via ST OMER. arrived at billet 2.30. handed up mule at billet left by No 3 sec 24 D.A.C.	
NOORDPEENE	7		Left billet at NOORDPEENE in morn 9.30 am CL Corpl TAPLIN Pte MILLIE with 10 sick horses in advance 9.30 am to ARNEKE & entrained same for NEUFCHATEL. Section passing through CASSEL arrived at STEENVOORDE 1.30 PM	
STEENVOORDE POPERINGHE	8		Left STEENVOORDE in morn 8.45 arrived at Billet POPERINGHE. 11.30 found barn	

WAR DIARY
or
INTELLIGENCE SUMMARY.
(Erase heading not required.)

Army Form C. 2118.

36th MOBILE VETERINARY SECTION
Date 8 Jan 16

Place	Date	Hour	Summary of Events and Information	Remarks and references to Appendices
POPERINGHE	JAN 8		& sleeping quarters in a disgraceful condition. men tidying up billet & horse lines for sick horses rest of day. 2 horses left behind by previous section 37 M.V.S.	
"	9		Draft from A.D.V.S. in morn 4 horses received for treatment. rain in morn	
	10		Fine day. 6 horses received for treatment. C.E. went to POPERINGHE re sick horse Corpl Yaplin & Pte Trillin returned from NEUFCHATEL in morn from evacuating	
	11		D.D.V.S. & A.D.V.S. called in morn. D.D.V.S. gave demonstration of new method of malleining to O.O's present Lt DONNWORTH, Lt HOTCHKISS, Lt MAC GREGOR & D.C. & A.D.V.S. present in office to a lecture 7 horses received for treatment. C.E. malleined 15 horses	
	12		wet & windy day, 8 horses received for treatment A.D.V.S. called in aft. Sgt APPLEBY & Pte PRIOR went to POPERINGHE to collect horse. C.E. malleined 12 horses	
	13		wet & windy day. 14 horses received for treatment, returned to unit. A.D.V.S. visited in aft. malleining out evacuation rolls in aft preparatory to evacuating next day to NO.13 VETY. HOSPITAL NEUFCHATEL	
	14		CORPL NUNN. PTE LEIPER IMREY & BROWN went with horses O.C. & men of section led horses down to POPERINGHE STATION. fine day 1 horse entered for treatment Pte Brown transferred to No 13 V HOSPITAL NEUFCHATEL O.C. MALLEINED 26 horses belonging to MOBILE VETY. SECTION.	

WAR DIARY
or
INTELLIGENCE SUMMARY.
(Erase heading not required.)

Army Form C. 2118.

Place	Date	Hour	Summary of Events and Information	Remarks and references to Appendices
POPERINGHE	JAN 15		Fine day. ADVS called in morn. 3 horses received for treatment	
"	16		Fine day 5 horses received for treatment. Corpl NUNN Ptes IMPEY & LEIPER returned from evacuating horses at NEUFCHATEL VETY. HOSPITAL. OC went away in morning & mustered horses of 74 Field amb.	
"	17		Fine day slight rain in aft. OC mustered horses of 74 Field Amb & Glasgow Yeomanry. horses (4) received for treatment	
"	18		Wet Day 2 horses received for treatment, ADVS called in morn. OC mustered 2 mules 74 Field ambulance Corpl TAPLIN, Pte WYLIE & Dr Hutchinson went with 28 horses to No 13 VETY HOSPITAL. NEUFCHATEL	
"	19		OC men of section entrained horses at POPERINGHE in morning. 7 horses received for treatment. ADVS called in morn. Men of section went to Butts (Divisional) in aft. windy day but fine	
"	20		Wet windy day. ADVS called in morn, men of section bury enemy cavalry horse to for sick horses. OC went down in aft to visit sick horse (broken leg) No 2 Sec. 24 DAC, horses (4) entered for treatment	
"	21		horses ( ) received for treatment. OC mustered horses in morn at Hdqrs RENINGHELST, men of section cavalry down to for transport horses. rainy & windy day. ADVS called in morn. men from Hi Sanitary Section put up incinerator. No mens of section helping with same. arrival in evening of No 662 SERGT BOARDMAN A.V.C. from No 5 Veterinary Hospital ABBEVILLE	

WAR DIARY or INTELLIGENCE SUMMARY

Army Form C. 2118.

36th MOBILE VETERINARY SECTION
Date 22 Jan 16

Place	Date	Hour	Summary of Events and Information	Remarks and references to Appendices
POPERINGHE	JAN 22		No 690 Sergt McDIARMETT, AVC transferred from 36 M.V.S. to No5 VETERINARY HOSPITAL ABBEVILLE left POPERINGHE STATION. 6 ANTRAIN. horses (2) entered for treatment, return of conducting party NEUFCHATEL CORPL. TAPLIN. PTE UPTON. & Dr HUTCHINSON men of section clipping horses morn & aft. windy & rain	
	23		Fine day 2 horses received for treatment. G.C. went down to RENINGHELST to Field Ambulance. men of section fried in aft. G.C. mallein'd horses of Div Hdqtrs in morn. men of section clipping horses in aft & morn.	
	24		Fine day mules of 24 Div Cyclist Company mallein'd in morn. horses received for treatment.	
	25		Fine day horses (18) received for treatment. 1 horse destroyed 108 Brigade Am Column Emaciation men of section clipping horses	
	26		Fine day dull. Sergt BOARDMAN. Pte PRIOR & PTE S. NOOKS went with 27 horses evacuated to No 13 VETY HOSPITAL NEUFCHATEL. G.C & crew of section entrained same at POPERINGHE STATION men of section clipping horses. horses (0) received for treatment rain in aft ADVS called in aft. horses (4) received for treatment, men of section clipping horses (transport) morn & aft	
	27		Wet morning (1) horses received for treatment return of Sergt BOARDMAN & Pte NOOKS from evacuating horses to NEUFCHATEL. Sgt APPLEBY went by train to HAZEBROUCK & returned in evening. men of section finished clipping horses in morn	
	28			

Army Form C. 2118.

WAR DIARY
or
INTELLIGENCE SUMMARY.
(Erase heading not required.)

Instructions regarding War Diaries and Intelligence Summaries are contained in F. S. Regs., Part II. and the Staff Manual respectively. Title pages will be prepared in manuscript.

36th MOBILE VETERINARY SECTION
Date 21.1.16

Place	Date	Hour	Summary of Events and Information	Remarks and references to Appendices
POPERINGHE	JAN 29		Horses (7) received for treatment, dull day, visit from the A.D.V.S. in morn.	
"	30th		Dull day(7) horses received for treatment including (2) cast horses.	
"	31st		Dull day (5) horses received for treatment, visit from ADVS in morn	

J. F. Harris Captain
O.C 36 Mobile Vety Section

24   36th Inftr: Vet: Sect:
        Vol: 6

WAR DIARY
INTELLIGENCE SUMMARY

Army Form C. 2118.

36th MOBILE VETERINARY SECTION

Place	Date	Hour	Summary of Events and Information	Remarks and references to Appendices
POPERINGHE	FEB 1		Horses (9) received for treatment. Fine day, frosty. (4) Cast horses received. Pte. PRIOR sentenced by ADVS to serve 28 days No1 Field Punishment on a charge of drunkenness. Prisoner to serve term under APM of this Division. Visit from DDVS. men of section paid. CE went to see horses.	
	2		Fine, frosty day. Horses (8) received for treatment. (1) Cast horse received. 41 Horses (including 8 cast by order DDR) evacuated to No 13 Vety Hospital. Corpl NUNN, Ptes MILLIER, GREEN & HALLET forming conducting party.	
	3		Fine day, windy, Horses (2) received for treatment. ADVS called in aft. Pte UPTON returned to section (at expiration of leave). Received communication from AVC HQrs stating that the delay of men belonging to Mobile Section in returning to unit when returning from hospital &c. was entirely the fault of 6 Co MVS, but in every case where men of this section have not returned in 48 hours it has been due to the horses being held up at Boulogne for a period of 12 to 16 hours necessitating them being kept in horses one day longer than is necessary for the trip. I have already written a complaint to ADVS who has forwarded it to D.D.V.S. II ARMY.	
	4 5		Wet day + windy (1) horses received for treatment. C.E attended sick animals of 72. Visit of D.D.V.T. who brought an experimental horse rug to be given a trial (2) horses received for treatment.	

WAR DIARY
or
INTELLIGENCE SUMMARY.

Army Form C. 2118.

Place	Date	Hour	Summary of Events and Information	Remarks and references to Appendices
POPERINGHE	Feb 7		Sent written application to ADVS for one months furlough in behalf of Sergt APPLEBY AVC on completion of 16 years service, but was informed by ADVS that this was not permissible although Authority (CRO No 559 31 Jan 1916) was granted (10) horses entered for treatment	
"	8		Visit by ADVS (9) horses entered for treatment	
"	9		Evacuated 26 horses to No 13 VETY HOSPITAL NEUFCHATEL (5) horses received for treatment	
	10		6 C treated horses of 73 Field Amb. 9 horses entered section	
	11		2 Horses entered section for treatment. wet day 1 horse destroyed (Syphic Arthritis Hock)	
	12		3 Horses entered section for treatment wet day. x	
	13		Visit from ADVS in aft. (4) horses received for treatment windy wet day.	
	14		7 horses entered for treatment	
	15		13 horses entered for treatment	
	16		Evacuated 36 horses to No 13 Vety Hospital NEUFCHATEL. 5 horses entered for treatment windy day.	
	17		Men of Section brushing bricks & missing concrete laying down same for aid horse stable.	
	18		2 horses entered for treatment	
			New finished slate floor in aft for sick horses. 3 horses entered for treatment	
	19		Pte Prior brought back from RENINGHELST in apt O.C. & Pte MILLIER went to 129 Co. R.H. M sick horse.	

Army Form C. 2118.

WAR DIARY
or
INTELLIGENCE SUMMARY.
(Erase heading not required.)

Instructions regarding War Diaries and Intelligence Summaries are contained in F. S. Regs., Part II. and the Staff Manual respectively. Title pages will be prepared in manuscript.

Place	Date	Hour	Summary of Events and Information	Remarks and references to Appendices
POPERINGHE	Feb 19 contd		3 horses entered for treatment.	
	20		O.C went to RENINGHELST in morn. Section paid in morn. horses entered for treatment	
	21		1 horses entered for treatment. ADVS called in morn.	
	22		11 horses entered for treatment. morn.	
	23		23 horses evacuated to No.13 Vety Hospital NEUFCHATEL arriv. 2 horses entered for treatment	
	24		horses entered for treatment. Visit from ADVS. in morn	
	25		No Horses entered for treatment Snow falling.	
	26		No Horses entered for treatment. Snow falling	
	27		A.D.V.S called in morn. 3 Horses entered for treatment	
	28		ADVS called in morn. 10 Horses entered for treatment.	
	29		ADVS called in morning 11 Horses entered for treatment	

[signature] Capt A.V.C
O.C 36 Mobile Vety Section

24 Dec

96 M vets
vol 7

Army Form C. 2118.

WAR DIARY
or
INTELLIGENCE SUMMARY.

(Erase heading not required.)

Instructions regarding War Diaries and Intelligence Summaries are contained in F. S. Regs., Part II. and the Staff Manual respectively. Title pages will be prepared in manuscript.

Place	Date	Hour	Summary of Events and Information	Remarks and references to Appendices
POPERINGHE	MAR 1		32 Horses evacuated to No 13 Vety Hospital NEUFCHATEL. 5 horses entered for treatment	Pte PRIOR evacuated sick
	2		4 horses entered for treatment. arrival of PTE PEACOCK & PTE TODD from No 3 Vety Hospital for duty with Section	
	3		5 horses entered for treatment	
	4		2 horses entered for treatment.	
	5		5 horses entered for treatment.	
	6		18 horses entered for treatment	
	7		14 horses entered for treatment	
	8		2 horses entered for treatment. 44 horses evacuated to No 13 Vety Hospital	Sgt Beaton. A.S.C. Driver INFEY.
			Arrived HAZEBROUCK in motor in exchanging limber G.S. for float. ADVS called in aft	
	9		— horses entered for treatment ADVS called in morn.	
	10		3 horses entered for treatment.	
	11		5 horses entered for treatment.	
	12		1 horses entered for treatment	
	13		4 horses entered for treatment	
	14		23 horses entered for treatment	

1577 Wt. W10791/1773 500,000 1/15 D. D. & L. A.D.S.S./Forms/C. 2118.

Army Form C. 2118.

WAR DIARY
or
INTELLIGENCE SUMMARY.
(Erase heading not required.)

Instructions regarding War Diaries and Intelligence Summaries are contained in F. S. Regs., Part II. and the Staff Manual respectively. Title pages will be prepared in manuscript.

Place	Date	Hour	Summary of Events and Information	Remarks and references to Appendices
POPERINGHE	MAR 15th		39 horses evacuated to No 13 Vety Hospital NEUFCHATEL. 18 horses entered for treatment	
"	16th		ADVS called in aft.	
"	17th		9 horses entered for treatment. 25 horses evacuated to No 13 Vety Hospital NEUFCHATEL. 8 horses received for treatment	
"	18th		Sn Impey returned with horse ambulance waggon from ABBEVILLE	
"	19th		Unit from the DDVS + ADVS action packing up preparatory to leaving 4 horses received for treatment	
"	20		1 horse received for treatment	
"	"		11 horses evacuated to No 13 Vety Hospital @ NEUFCHATEL. 2 horses received for treatment	
"	"		Sn IMPEY 35456 left on leave. men packing up mom & aft.	
FLETRE	21st		36 Mobile Vet section left billet 8:30 AM Via BOESCHEPE & GOUDVAERSVELDE. FLETRE arrived new billet 1:30 PM. ADVS called in aft. 2 horses left by CANADIAN MVS	
"	22		Section fitting up new billet . 1 horse received for treatment. return of conducting party from NEUFCHATEL	
"	23		2 horses received for treatment	
"	24		4 horses entered for treatment ADVS called in morn. Horses collected from Herdeghem in ambulance	
"	25		2 horses entered for treatment. Section fitting up shelter for sick horses	
"	26		horses received for treatment	

Army Form C. 2118

WAR DIARY
or
INTELLIGENCE SUMMARY

(Erase heading not required.)

Instructions regarding War Diaries and Intelligence Summaries are contained in F. S. Regs., Part II. and the Staff Manual respectively. Title Pages will be prepared in manuscript.

Place	Date	Hour	Summary of Events and Information	Remarks and references to Appendices
FLETRE	Mar 27		- horses entered for treatment.	
	28		4 " "	
	29		2 " "	
	30		Evacuated 4 horses to No 13 Vety Hospital	
	31		15 horses evacuated to No 13 Vety Hospital NCO & 1 man i/c of Sgt Boardman & horses entered for treatment	

B. Marin Capt. A.V.C.
O.C. 36 Mobile Vety Section

1875 Wt. W593/826 1,000,000 4/15 J.B.C. & A. A.D.S.S./Forms/C. 2118.

WAR DIARY or INTELLIGENCE SUMMARY

Army Form C. 2118.

Place	Date	Hour	Summary of Events and Information	Remarks and references to Appendices
FLETRE.	APRIL 1		36th Mobile Vety Section left billet at COQ DE PAILLE 8AM arrived new billet 11.30 B.1.D.6.& myf	
NIEPPE.	2		36 left two horses behind 1/c of Pte Bastin 00S men of section filling up but roadway etc.	
			1 horse entered for treatment ADVS called in apt.	
	3		2 horses entered for treatment	
	4		9 horses entered for treatment, men filling up entrance to billet roadway etc. Sgt Board left on 1 months furlough.	
	5		2 horses entered for treatment	
	6		2 horses entered for treatment	
	7		2 horses received for treatment	
			12 horses evacuated to No 13 Vety Hospital NEUFCHATEL. 1/c Sgt NUNN PLEUPTON. return of Sgt BENTON from leave. 4 horses entered for treatment	
	8		2 horses received for treatment	
	9		No horses received. return of bricklaying party from NEUFCHATEL.	
	10		5 horses received for treatment	
	11		1 horse received for treatment	
	12		Cpl TAPLIN left for ENGLAND for leave. 3 horses received for treatment A.D.V.S. called in apt.	
	13		9 horses received for treatment	

WAR DIARY
or
INTELLIGENCE SUMMARY.

(Erase heading not required.)

Army Form C. 2118.

36th MOBILE VETERINARY SECTION
Date 14·4·16

Place	Date	Hour	Summary of Events and Information	Remarks and references to Appendices
NIEPPE	April 14		14 Horses Evacuated to No 13 V.H. NEUFCHATEL 1/c of NCO & 1 man 6 horses entered for treatment	
	15		return of Pt. WRIGHT from Base, most from A.B.V.S.	
	16		return of Conducting party from NEUFCHATEL	
	17		4 horses received for treatment	
	18		" " " "	
	19		" evacuated 16 horses to No 13 V.H. NEUFCHATEL 1/c of Cpt.. B.O. & 1 man	
	20		" " new journey RSPCA ambulance	
	21		" " " "	
	22		" " " "	
	23		" " " "	
	24		" " " "	
	25		" " 21 horses evacuated to No 13 V.H. NEUFCHATEL 1/c of NCO & 2 men	
	26		" " A.D.V.S. called in morn.	
	27		O.C. 36 M.V.S. started for England on leave. Capt. BLACKBURN 2nd vet taken in absence of O.C.	
	28		7 horses received for treatment Evacuated 16 horses No 13 V.H. NEUFCHATEL 1/c Sgt. BENTON. & 2 men	
	29		A.D.V.S. called.	
	30		2 horses received for treatment	

J. Blackburn
Capt. A.V.C. for O.C. 36 M.V.S.

Army Form C. 2118.

WAR DIARY
or
INTELLIGENCE SUMMARY.
(Erase heading not required.)

Vol. 9
XXIV

36th MOBILE VETERINARY SECTION
Date 1.5.16

Place	Date	Hour	Summary of Events and Information	Remarks and references to Appendices
NIEPPE	MAY 1		18 Horses received for treatment A.D.V.S. called	
"	2		11 Horses received for treatment. 31 Horses evacuated to No 13 V.H. NEUFCHATEL. I/c of S/S NUNN & 4 men	
"	3		5 Horses received for treatment	
"	4		Visit of A.D.V.S. & D.D.V.S. 3 horses received for treatment 8 Horses evacuated to No 13 V.H. NEUFCHATEL. I/c of Sgt BOARDMAN	
"	5		5 Horses received for treatment. Visit from A.D.V.S.	
"	6		Return of O.C. from leave ENGLAND Return of Sgt Boardman for treatment	
"	7		— Horses received for treatment	
"	8		12 Horses received for treatment	
"	9		2 Horses received for treatment 28 Horses evacuated to No 13 V.H. NEUFCHATEL. I/c of Sgt BENTON & 3 men.	
"	10		Visit from A.D.V.S.	
"	11		1 Horse received for treatment	
"	12		7 Horses received for treatment Return of Conducting party from NEUFCHATEL	
"	12		3 Horses received for treatment A.D.V.S. called in morn	
"	13		3 Horses received for treatment	

Army Form C. 2118.

WAR DIARY
or
INTELLIGENCE SUMMARY.
(Erase heading not required.)

Instructions regarding War Diaries and Intelligence Summaries are contained in F. S. Regs., Part II. and the Staff Manual respectively. Title pages will be prepared in manuscript.

36th MOBILE VETERINARY SECTION
Date 14·5·16

Place	Date	Hour	Summary of Events and Information	Remarks and references to Appendices
NIEPPE	MAY 14		2 Horses received for treatment	
	15		1 " " " "	
	16		1 " " " " 16 Horses evacuated to No 13 V.H. NEUFCHATEL. 25 to convalescent farm.	
	17		6 " " " "	
	18		1 " " " " return of conducting party from NEUFCHATEL	
	19		3 " " " " A D.V.S called in morn.	
	20		3 " " " "	
	21		1 " " " "	
	22		8 " " " " A.D.V.S called in morn	
	23		4 " " " " 22 Horses evacuated to No 13 V H NEUFCHATEL i/c Sgt BOARDMAN & 2 men	
			Pte G.E.E.W. S.E No 8795 reported for duty from No 4 V.H. CALAIS.	
	24		1 Horse received for treatment	
	25		1 " " " " return of conducting party from NEUFCHATEL.	
	26		3 " " " "	
	27		4 " " " " Sgt APPLEBY. Proceeded to BIRMINGHAM on one months furlough.	
	28		2 " " " "	

Army Form C. 2118.

WAR DIARY
or
INTELLIGENCE SUMMARY.
(Erase heading not required.)

Instructions regarding War Diaries and Intelligence Summaries are contained in F. S. Regs., Part II and the Staff Manual respectively. Title pages will be prepared in manuscript.

36th MOBILE VETERINARY SECTION
Date 24/5/16

Place	Date	Hour	Summary of Events and Information	Remarks and references to Appendices
NIEPPE	MAY 29		7 Horses received for treatment	
"	30		22 horses evacuated to No 13 Vety. Hospital. Neufchatel.	
			1/c Sgt BENTON & 2 men	
"	31		3 horses received for treatment. C/L NUNN left for ENGLAND 9 days leave.	

Captn. AVC
OC 36 Mobile Vety Sectn.

36. M. Vet. Sec.
Vol 10

Army Form C. 2118.

WAR DIARY
or
INTELLIGENCE SUMMARY.
(Erase heading not required.)

XXIV

Place	Date	Hour	Summary of Events and Information	Remarks and references to Appendices
			June	
NIEPPE	JUNE 1.		7 horses received for treatment	
	2.		" " " " " " Visit from ADVS. Full marching order Parade held in aft by O.C.	
	3.		" " " " " " Visit from D.D.V.S. rifle inspection in afternoon.	
	4.		" " " " " "	
	5.		" " " " " " Visit from ADVS.	
	6.		" " " " " " 45 Horses evacuated to No 13 Vety Hospital NEUFCHATEL I/c of Sgt BENTON & 4 men.	
	6 cont'd			
	7.		" " " " " "	
	8.		" " " " " " Capt Lawrie & Sgt BOARDMAN went to BAILLEUL for instructions in new method of putting gas helmets, return of conducting party NCO & 4 men from NEUFCHATEL	
	9.		Horses received for treatment. Visit from ADVS Sgt BENTON & evacuated 22 horses to No 13 Vety Hospital NEUFCHATEL. DVS. DDVS. & ADVS visited section in aft. & inspects horses billets etc	
	10		3 Horses received for treatment.	
	11		2 Horses received for treatment. On Sunday afternoon a Mounted Parade ensembly of 16 Mounted men & 3 Horses with Waggons, belonging to the Section - 6 Prizes being given. Judges Lt-Col Doyle D.S.O.	

Army Form C. 2118.

WAR DIARY
or
INTELLIGENCE SUMMARY.
(Erase heading not required.)

Instructions regarding War Diaries and Intelligence Summaries are contained in F. S. Regs., Part II. and the Staff Manual respectively. Title pages will be prepared in manuscript.

Place	Date	Hour	Summary of Events and Information	Remarks and references to Appendices
	JUNE			
	11 Contd		AA&MG 24 Division. Lt Col WILSON. CMG. DDVS 2nd ARMY, & Major LEANING ADVS 24th Division.	
	12		In the Armms of the Judges the turn out was a marked success.	
			11 Horses received for treatment	
	13		Visit by AA&QMG. 26 Horses evacuated to No 13 Vety Hospital NEUFCHATEL. Nurgmate 1/c Cpl NIVEN & 3 men.	
	14		2 Horses received for treatment, return of Pte. ROGERS from leave.	
	15		2 Horses received for treatment	
	16		5 Horses " " "	
	17		4 Horses " " "	
	18		1 " " " "	Visit from ADVS in morning.
	19		19 " " " "	
	20		5 " " " "	33 Horses evacuated to No 13 VH No 13 VH. 1/c Sgt BENTON & 3 men
	21		5 " " " "	
	22		" " " " "	Return of conducting party from No 13 V.H. NEUFCHATEL. Visit from ADVS.
	23		" " " " "	3 Horses evacuated to No 13. VH NEUFCHATEL 1/c of 1 man (NCO)
	24		9 " " " "	

1577 Wt. W10791/1773 500,000 1/15 D. D. & L.   A.D.S.S./Forms/C. 2118.

WAR DIARY
or
INTELLIGENCE SUMMARY.

(Erase heading not required.)

Army Form C. 2118.

Place	Date	Hour	Summary of Events and Information	Remarks and references to Appendices
NIEPPE	June 25		Horses received for treatment Cpl NUNN & 6 men evacuated 16 horses by road to V.H. ST.OMER.	
	26.		return of Sgt APPLEBY from ENGLAND 28 days leave. Return of men from NO 13 V.H NEUFCHATEL	
	27.		14 Horses received for treatment	
	28.		11 " " " 15 horses evacuated to NO 13 V.H. NEUFCHATEL i/c of Sgt BOARDMAN & 1 man	
			5 " " " Pte MATTLESS left for ENGLAND 8 days leave visit from A.D.V.S.	
	29		return of conducting party from ST.OMER. i/c of CPL.NUNN. 6 men.	
	30		return of conducting party from NEUFCHATEL, Sgt & 1 man visit from A.D.V.S	
			8 Horses received for treatment	

Captn. A.V.C
OC. 36 Mobile Vety Sectn.

WAR DIARY
or
INTELLIGENCE SUMMARY.
(Erase heading not required.)

Army Form C.2118
24 of July
36th MOBILE VETERINARY SECTION
Date 1.7.16
VOL II

Instructions regarding War Diaries and Intelligence Summaries are contained in F.S. Regs., Part II. and the Staff Manual respectively. Title pages will be prepared in manuscript.

Place	Date	Hour	Summary of Events and Information	Remarks and references to Appendices
R.NIEPPE	JULY 1st		4 Horses received for treatment. Visit from ADVS. Small arms Inspection 2.30 PM	
	2nd		2 " " " 22 Horses evacuated to St.OMER. No 23 VH I/c Sgt APPLEBY	
	3		4 5 men by road.	
	4		4 Horses received for treatment.	
	5		C.C. rode over to LOCRE in search of new billet. Horses received for treatment. Men of Section fixing up limber in aft. Section clearing up preparatory to moving next day. 2 horses taken up to NO 52 MVS.	
Nr BAILLEUL	6		36 MVS left billet for new location Nr BAILLEUL with sick horses & waggons arrived at billet about 10am. Running out have linis etc Visit from ADVS in morning	
"	7		Horses received for treatment 3	
"	8		Horses received for treatment 5	
"	9		Horses received for treatment 9 Visit from ADVS.	
"	10		Horses received for treatment. 16 Horses evacuated by road to St.OMER. no 23 Vety Hospl I I/c of Cpl NUNN & 4 men.	
LE SEAU	11th		Section down up preparatory to moving next day. Horses received for treatment. Section left Br'lt at BAILLEUL & returned to old billet at LE SEAU nr NIEPPE 10.30 AM B.I.D. 9.3	

1577 Wt. W10791/1773 500,000 1/15 D.D.&L. A.D.S.S./Forms/C. 2118.

Army Form C. 2118.

WAR DIARY
or
INTELLIGENCE SUMMARY.
(Erase heading not required.)

Instructions regarding War Diaries and Intelligence Summaries are contained in F. S. Regs., Part II. and the Staff Manual respectively. Title pages will be prepared in manuscript.

36th MOBILE VETERINARY SECTION
Date 11.7.16

Place	Date	Hour	Summary of Events and Information	Remarks and references to Appendices
LE SEAU NR NIEPPE	July 11 continued		men picking up lime lime for sick animals & mange cases horses (10) received for treatment A.D.V.S. visited in aft.	
	12		5 Horses received for treatment	
	13		4 " " " " Visit from A.D.V.S.	
	14		3 " " " "	
	15		Rifle Inspection in morning. Horses received for treatment. 6 horses sent to ESTAIRES for boat to ST OMER. 9 to 23 VETY. HOSPITAL.	
	16		Horses ( ) received for treatment. 58 horses evacuated to No 23 Vety Hospital ST OMER. 1/c Sgt BOARD 1 N.V Sgt BENTON & 10 men. by road visit from A.D.V.S. in afternoon.	
	17		Horses evacuated Horses entered for treatment (5). 11 horses evacuated by boat 1/c of Sgt Appleby. Pte WILLIAMS V MATTLESS	
	18		10 Horses received for treatment	
	19		3 Horses received for treatment 6 horses evacuated by boat.	
	20		Horses received for treatment 5 Horses evacuated to No 32 M.V.S. previous to 36 M.V.S leaving for new billet.	
	21		1 Horse received for treatment 36 M.V.S. left billet for COG. DE. PAILLE near FLETRE 5 A.M. arrived at new billet 11.30 a.m. men picking up loose lines etc, 12 horses evacuated to ST OMER by road 1/c M.L NUNN & 3 men. visit from D.D.V.S. & A.D.V.S.	

1577 Wt. W10791/1773 500,000 1/15 D. D. & L. A.D.S.S./Forms/C. 2118.

Army Form C. 2118.

WAR DIARY
or
INTELLIGENCE SUMMARY.
(Erase heading not required.)

Instructions regarding War Diaries and Intelligence Summaries are contained in F. S. Regs., Part II. and the Staff Manual respectively. Title pages will be prepared in manuscript.

36th MOBILE VETERINARY SECTN — Date 22 JULY

Place	Date	Hour	Summary of Events and Information	Remarks and references to Appendices
COQ DE TAILLE	July 22		3 horses received for treatment	
	23		4 " " " "	
	24		5 " " " "	
	25		5 horses evacuated to No 52. M.V.S. 1/c of Sgt + 2 men	
			6 horses evacuated to No 40 MVS 31.D.9.3 fleet 26 1/c Sgt + 2 men	
			36 MVS left billet at COQ DE BAILLE & entrained at BAILLEUL WEST. left 5.30 P.M. arrived at	
CAVILLON	26	2 AM	AMIENS 2 AM left station 3. AM arrived CAVILLON 9.45 AM. 2 horses received for treatment	
"	27		11. Horses received " treatment	
"	28		12. Horses " " "	
"	29		23 horses evacuated to No 7 V.H. FORGES LES EAUX. 1/c Sgt BOARDMAN + 2 men	
CAVILLON	30		9 horses received " treatment	
	31		10 " " " "	
		9.30 a.m.	arrived at CORBIE 7 P.M. through AMIENS	
			Men packing up preparatory to leaving & subsequently left CAVILLON	

Captn. A. V. C.
O.36 Mobile Vety Sectn

Army Form C. 2118.

WAR DIARY
or
INTELLIGENCE SUMMARY.
(Erase heading not required.)

Instructions regarding War Diaries and Intelligence Summaries are contained in F. S. Regs., Part II. and the Staff Manual respectively. Title pages will be prepared in manuscript.

36th MOBILE VETERINARY SECTION
Date Sept 1916

Place	Date	Hour	Summary of Events and Information	Remarks and references to Appendices
CORBIE	Aug 1st		5 Horses received in return. 13 horses evacuated to FORGES LES EAUX 1/c of Sgt Benbi & 1 man	
N.BRAY	2		Section left CORBIE in a.m. 3:30 arrived at billet about 7.30 p.m. in absolute bare ground no buildings of any description in same.	
BOIS d. TAILLES	3		Section after dinner 2.p.m. shifted billet into area occupied by 30th Division	
	4			
	5		16 Horses evacuated to No 7 V Hospital FORGES les EAUX.	
	6			
	7			
	8		22 Horses evacuated to No 7 V Hospital FORGES. les EAUX	
	9			
	10			
	11			
	12			
MEAULTE	13		36 M.V.S. left billet at BOIS. de TAILLES at 3 PM arrived at billet near MEAULTE	
	14			
	15		16 Horses Evacuated to No 7 V.H. FORGES. les EAUX	

Army Form C. 2118.

24 Vol 12

WAR DIARY
or
INTELLIGENCE SUMMARY.

(Erase heading not required.)

36th MOBILE VETERINARY SECTION
Date Sept. 1916

Instructions regarding War Diaries and Intelligence Summaries are contained in F. S. Regs., Part II. and the Staff Manual respectively. Title pages will be prepared in manuscript.

Place	Date	Hour	Summary of Events and Information	Remarks and references to Appendices
MEAULTE	August 16			
"	17		Left billet & arrived in new billet in main street MEAULTE (64 HIGH STREET) vacated by 55 MVS	
"	18			
"	19		24 Horses evacuated to No 7 VH FORGES LES EAUX.	
"	20			
"	21			
"	22		29 Horses evacuated to No 7 VH.	
"	23			
"	24		53 Horses evacuated to No 7. VH.	
"	25			
"	26			
"	27			
"	28			
"	29		28 Horses evacuated to No 7 VH.	
"	30			
"	31			

[signature]
Captn. AVC
OO 36 Mobile Vety Sectn

24 Army Form C. 2118. Vol 13

WAR DIARY
or
INTELLIGENCE SUMMARY.
(Erase heading not required.)

Instructions regarding War Diaries and Intelligence Summaries are contained in F. S. Regs., Part II. and the Staff Manual respectively. Title pages will be prepared in manuscript.

36th MOBILE VETERINARY SECTION
Date September 1916

Place	Date	Hour	Summary of Events and Information	Remarks and references to Appendices
	September 1916			
MEAULTE	1		32 Horses evacuated to No 7 V.H. FORGES les EAUX. I/c 1 Sgt & 2 men	
"	2			
"	3			
"	4		39 horses evacuated to No 7 V H FORGES. LES. EAUX. I/c of B/fl. & 4 men	
"	5		Section packing up preparatory to moving	
"	6		32 Horses evacuated to No 7 V.H. FORGES les EAUX. I/c of Sgt & 2 men	
LONGPRE	7		36 MVS left billet 12.40 a.m via BUIRE. DAOURS. AMIENS. billeted for night at LONGPRÉ ET AMIENS. 2.40 p.m	
AILLY le haut Clocher	8		Section left 2m LONGPRE 6.45 a.m arrived at AILLY le haut Clocher. about 5.10 p.m	
	9			
	10			
	11			
	12			
	13			
	14		Evacuated by road 20 Horses to No 22 V.H. ABBEVILLE	
	15			
	16		Evacuated by road 9 horses to No 2 V H ABBEVILLE.	

WAR DIARY or **INTELLIGENCE SUMMARY**

Army Form C. 2118.

(Erase heading not required.)

Instructions regarding War Diaries and Intelligence Summaries are contained in F. S. Regs., Part II and the Staff Manual respectively. Title pages will be prepared in manuscript.

Place	Date	Hour	Summary of Events and Information	Remarks and references to Appendices
	September			
AILLY	17		O.C. Regt Affleby & Lyt Munro collected sick horses from various localities PICQUIGNY. BELLOY-SUR-SOMME	
"	18		CONDE-FOLIE left by units	
"	18		Section getting ready for moving PIE REYNOLDS from No 14 H reported for duty with 36 M.V.S	
PONT-REMY	19	9.26 P.M	36 M.V.S left billet. entrained at PONT REMY. 12.0 a.m 5 horses evacuated by road from AILLY to ABBEVILLE.	V.H. No 22
PERNES	20	5.30 a.m	section detrained at PERNES 5.30 f a.m	
"	21			
"	22			
BRUAY	23	5.30 A.M	36 MVS left billet at PERNES & arrived at BRUAY, about 11.15 a.m	
	24			
	25			
FRESNICOURT	26	5.30 A.M	Section left BRUAY. 5.30 A.M arrived at FRESNICOURT taking over billet of 21 MVS 9th DIVISION.	
"	27		although this billet has been occupied by Mobile Vety Sections for over a year, no improvements whatever have been made	
"	28			
"	29			
"	30		during the past week the Section has been extremely busy preparing billet for winter quarters	

[signature] Captn. A.V.C
O.C 36 Mobile Vety Sectn

Army Form C. 2118.

M.V.S. Vol 14

WAR DIARY
or
INTELLIGENCE SUMMARY.

(Erase heading not required.)

Place	Date	Hour	Summary of Events and Information	Remarks and references to Appendices
FRESNICOURT	October 1			
	2			
	3		Sgt IDILL AVC reported for duty with 36 M.V.S.	
	4			
	5		74 Horses Evacuated to No 13 Vety Hospital	
	6			
	7		63 Horses Evacuated to No 13 Vety Hospital	
	8			
	9			
	10		86 Horses Evacuated to No 13 Vety Hospital	
	11			
	12			
	13		87 horses evacuated to No 13 Vety Hospital	
	14			
	15			
	16		80 Horses evacuated to No 13 Vety Hospital, Return men clipping horses.	

WAR DIARY
or
INTELLIGENCE SUMMARY.

Army Form C. 2118.

Place	Date	Hour	Summary of Events and Information	Remarks and references to Appendices
FRESNICOURT	Oct 17-27		Section extremely busy hauling material, building approaches, floors for winter shelters.	
	Oct 27		Evacuated 80 horses, nearly all of which were Artillery cases from 24th Divisional Artillery.	
	28		The Section was relieved by 1st Canadian M.V.S.	
BRUAY	28		The Section took up Billets at Bruay & remained there until the 30th.	
DROUVIN	30		On the 30th the Section relieved the #6th Division M.V.S. at Drouvin, also took over 13 horses from them.	
	31		The Section again resumed building for winter comfort.	

J Mann Capt. A.V.C.
O.C. 36 Mobile Vety Section

24

Army Form C. 2118.

WAR DIARY
or
INTELLIGENCE SUMMARY.
(Erase heading not required.)

Instructions regarding War Diaries and Intelligence Summaries are contained in F. S. Regs., Part II. and the Staff Manual respectively. Title pages will be prepared in manuscript.

Place	Date	Hour	Summary of Events and Information	Remarks and references to Appendices
DROUVIN	Nov 1			
	2			
	3			
	4			
	5			
	6			
	7			
	8			
	9			
	10			
	11		Evacuated 25 horses to No 13 V.H.	
	12			
	13			
	14		Evacuated horses to No 13 V.H.	
	15			
	16			
	17			

1577 Wt.W10791/1773 500,000 1/15 D.D.&L.   A.D.S.S./Forms/C. 2118.

Army Form C. 2118.

WAR DIARY
or
INTELLIGENCE SUMMARY.
(Erase heading not required.)

36th MOBILE
Date NOVEMBER
VETERINARY SECTION

Place	Date	Hour	Summary of Events and Information	Remarks and references to Appendices
DROUVIN	NOV 18		Sgt BETHEL AVC (temp. duty with 36 MVS transferred to 25th Bde RFA 8th Division	
"	19		Sgt TOON AVC " " " " L Bty 107 Bde RFA 24 Division	
"	20		Sgt TURNELL AVC " " " " No 3 Section 24 Division	
"	21		The Band of 24 Division played at billet of 36 MVS in aft. 2 till 4. Recruit reported from Chief Constable MANCHESTER of (accidentally killed) PTE GREENER 5089 AVC 36 MVS on leave in ENGLAND 15.11.16.	
"	22		N 5023 Pte GODDEN A AVC proceeded to ENGLAND on leave. (FOLKESTONE	
"	23			
"	24			
"	25		C.C. 36 MVS. I.N C096 men including Ambulance proceeded to RELY for temporary evacuation of horses of 1st CORPS.	
"	26		8 NO 4263 Sgt I DILL AVC returned from leave to ENGLAND. N 5661 Pte HALLETT proceeded on leave (27.11.16) to BRIXTON LONDON.	
"	27. 28			

Army Form C. 2118.

WAR DIARY
or
INTELLIGENCE SUMMARY.
(Erase heading not required.)

Instructions regarding War Diaries and Intelligence Summaries are contained in F. S. Regs., Part II. and the Staff Manual respectively. Title pages will be prepared in manuscript.

Place	Date	Hour	Summary of Events and Information	Remarks and references to Appendices
DROUVIN	NOV 29		Return of O.C. NCO & from RELY. (from warworking horse)	
	30		Report of Itinerary of Detachment, sent to ADVS. 24 Division	

B. Lewis
Captain O.C.
OC 36 Mobile, Vety. Sectn

36TH MOBILE
NOVEMBER 30, 16.
VETERINARY SECTN

Army Form C. 2118.

WAR·DIARY
or
INTELLIGENCE SUMMARY.
(Erase heading not required.)

26th MOBILE VETERINARY SECTION Date December

Vol 16

Place	Date	Hour	Summary of Events and Information	Remarks and references to Appendices
DROUVIN	DEC 1		2 Cases of Lstr. painting horse ambulance	
	2		29 Horses evacuated to No 13 Vety Hospital NEUFCHATEL	
	3			
	4		Pte GODDEN·A·AVC returned from leave	
	5			
	6		C.B. 1st/50 & 6 men with Ambulance left for MONCHY·BRETON in evening. Cpl MILLIER departed for England on leave	
	7		Sgt BENTON & 3 men evacuated 33 horses to No 13 Vety Hospital NEUFCHATEL	
	8		Dr HOGAN·(DIVTRAIN) departed for England on leave.	
	9		return of conducting party from NEUFCHATEL	
	10		Evacuated 24 Horses No 13 VETY HOSPITAL. NEUFCHATEL Cpl WHITCHURCH & 2 men	
	11		return of conducting party from NEUFCHATEL	
	12		Horse waggon ordered also for clerk from in oft.	
	13			
	14		20 Horses Evacuated to No 13 Vety Hospital NEUFCHATEL i/c Sergt I DILL 9 men	
	15			

Army Form C. 2118.

WAR DIARY
or
INTELLIGENCE SUMMARY.
(Erase heading not required.)

Instructions regarding War Diaries and Intelligence Summaries are contained in F. S. Regs., Part II. and the Staff Manual respectively. Title pages will be prepared in manuscript.

36th MOBILE
Date December 31.1916
VETERINARY SEC[TION]

Place	Date	Hour	Summary of Events and Information	Remarks and references to Appendices
DROUVIN	DEC 16			
	17		No 4263 Sergt. I. DILL W.H. AVC 36 MVS transferred to No 5 MVS 5 Division & No 5926 a/Sergt BENTON W.C. confirmed from AVC BASE RECORDS 1.12.16.	
	18			
	19			
	20			
	21		Evacuated 45 horses to No 13 V.H. NEUFCHATEL. 1/c C/Sgt MILLIER & 3 men.	
	22			
	23			
	24			
	25			
	26		Evacuated 27 horses No 13 V.H. NEUFCHATEL. 1/c C/Sgt ROGERS & 2 men	
	27			
	28			
	29			
	30			
	31		Entire Section including C.C. went through gas drill w apft. all helmets tested in gassed room	

Captn AVC
OC 36 Mobile. Vety Sec tn

Army Form C. 2118.

WAR DIARY
or
INTELLIGENCE SUMMARY
(Erase heading not required.)

Vol 77

Place	Date	Hour	Summary of Events and Information	Remarks and references to Appendices
DROUVIN	1917 JAN 1st		ADVS called in afternoon, limber waggon carting stone from NOEUX LES MINES for stable floors.	
	2nd		Evacuated 36 horses to No 13 Vety Hospital NEUFCHATEL. 1/c of 1 Sergt & 3 men.	
	3		Limber waggon carting stone for stable floor in aft.	
			Limber waggon carting stone for sick lines. 3 men (reinforcements) arrived for duty viz: 36 MVS from Hq Vety Hospital "DIEPPE" Pte EAGLE.H. Pte LOTT.A. & Pte POWELL. Shifting sick horses	
	4		Limber waggon carting stone for sick lines. Man & aft. Shifting sick horses.	
	5		Evacuated 20 horses to NO 13 VH NEUFCHATEL 1/c of L/Cpl & 1 man. 2 trips to station with float.	
	6		Limber waggon carting stone for stables. Men shifting sick horses	
	7		Limber waggon carting stone for stables. Men shifting sick horses	
	8		Small arms inspection in aft of section by O.C. Men shifting sick horses. Return of branding party in afternoon. Return of Dr A HUTCHINSON from ENGLAND (on leave)	
	9		Horse & shifting of sick horses man & aft. Return of Pte SNOOK. AVC. 36 MVS from ENGLAND (on leave)	
	10		Shifting Section horses man & aft	
	11		Horse clipping of Section horses man & aft	
	12		Evacuated 32 horses to NEUFCHATEL 1/c L/Cpl ROGERS & 3 men. Horse shifting of Section horses	
	13		Limber waggon carting stone for stable floors.	

1577 Wt. W10791/1773 500,000 1/15 D. D. & L. A.D.S.S./Forms/C. 2118.

Army Form C. 2118.

WAR DIARY
or
INTELLIGENCE SUMMARY.
(Erase heading not required.)

Instructions regarding War Diaries and Intelligence Summaries are contained in F. S. Regs., Part II. and the Staff Manual respectively. Title pages will be prepared in manuscript.

Place	Date 1917	Hour	Summary of Events and Information	Remarks and references to Appendices
DROUVIN	Jany 14		Waggon carting straw for stables etc	
	15		" " return of conducting party from NEUFCHATEL	
	16		" " NO 735609 Dr HUTCHINSON T. ASC proceeded to ASC Depot	
	"		(H T & S) HAVRE. Transferred from No 36 Mobile Vety Section	
	17		No 5661 Pte HALLETT. W. AVC. 36 MVS proceeded to No 2 Veterinary Hospital HAVRE, transferred from No 36 Mobile Veterinary Section.	
	18		Divisional sign painted on limber waggon in morn.	
	19		Evacuated 15 horses to No 18 Vety Hospital NEUFCHATEL I/c of Sgt & 4 men	
	20			
	21		No 747 Sergt YOUNGMAN. H.E. AVC reported to 36 MVS (temporary duty with MVS)	
	22		return of conducting party from NEUFCHATEL	
	23		OC infected horses of 24 Divisional Training Battalion for contagious Diseases in aft.	
	24		Arms Inspection of men of Section in aft.	
	25			
	26		Evacuated 15 horses to No 13 VH NEUFCHATEL I/c C/H MILLIER & 1 man. & 707 Sergt YOUNGMAN. H.E. AVC	
	26		proceeded on duty to 121 Hy Bty R.G.A. 50th HAG.	

WAR DIARY
or
INTELLIGENCE SUMMARY.
(Erase heading not required.)

Army Form C. 2118.

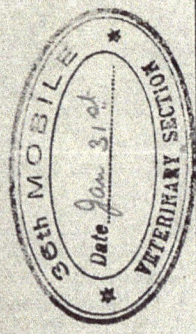

Place	Date	Hour	Summary of Events and Information	Remarks and references to Appendices
DROUVIN	JANY 27. 28. 29. 30. 31		Return of Conducting Party from NEUFCHATEL.	

Captⁿ. AVC
OC 36 Mobile Vety Sectⁿ

WAR DIARY
or
INTELLIGENCE SUMMARY.
(Erase heading not required.)

Army Form C. 2118.

Place	Date	Hour	Summary of Events and Information	Remarks and references to Appendices
DROUVIN	FEBY 1		5 Horses treated with Balsam Sulfide (for mange)	
	2		O.C. went to BRAQUEMONT to A.D.V.S. in morning	
	3		J.S. wagon carting also for slaughter	
	4		" No 3512 Pte HALL.G. from No 23 Veterinary Hospital admitted for duty to 36 Mobile Vety Section	
	5		O.C. went down to A.D.V.S office (in absence of A.D.V.S.on leave in ENGLAND)	
	6		O.C. went to A.D.V.S office in aft. 51 to 74 went Ambulance to collect horses	
	7		Rifle Inspection of Horse Exchange completion in aft. hand of Section paid in aft.	
	8		O.C. went to A.D.V.S office in afternoon	
	9		O.C. went to A.D.V.S office in afternoon	
	10		Evacuated 40 horses to No 13 V H NEUFCHATEL i/c of left 43 men. O.C. went to A.D.V.S office in morning	
	10		O.C went to A.D.V.S office to see A.D.V.S of 37 Division at H.Q. in aft. reference moving No 5170	
			Sergt PLUMLEY.H.AV.C. from D Bty 107 R.S.A. transferred from D.107. to 36 MVS (for temporary duty)	
	11		O.C went to H.Q. & also to BETHUNE re billets for 36 MVS.	
			Section all hacking up, loading waggon preparatory to moving	
	12		Evacuated 19 sick horses from BETHUNE STN for No 13 VH i/c Sgt & 1 men. Return of Conducting party from NEUFCHATEL.	

WAR DIARY or INTELLIGENCE SUMMARY.

Army Form C. 2118.

Place	Date	Hour	Summary of Events and Information	Remarks and references to Appendices
ECQUEDECQUES	F'EBY 13	8·AM	36 Mobile Vety Section left Billet at DROUVIN, proceeded to new billet at ECQUEDECQUES. VIA FOUQUEREUIL. CHOCQUES. LILLERS arrived at billet 11·30 a.m. 1 horse left behind at DROUVIN il of No 26 M.V.S. 37 Division. in oft men fixing up stables. horse lines & billets	
	14		C.C. went up to H.Q. to A.D.V.S. at LA BRUVIERE. in morn.	
	15		Return of conducting party from NEUFCHATEL. C.C went to A.D.V.S in morning. Ammo Inspection of foot drill in oft. men of section paid	
	16		C.C. went to A.D.V.S. in morning. Dr. WILLIAMS. A.S.C returned from LaventHie morning. PTE SNOOKA. Ave Riche. to 72 Yd Ambulance in morn. C.B.A. NCO went to ALLOUAGNE to see about advanced Collecting Station. 504 PTE SNOOKA·AVC. 36 MVS evacuated to No 23 CCS.	
	17		C.C. went to ADVS Office at LABRUVIERE in morn. ADVS returned from leave to ENGLAND	
	18		C.C. 36 MVS left LILLERS at 1·30 for leave to ENGLAND. Capt BLACKBURN. AVC taking over temporary command of Section during absence of CC.	
	19		A.D.V.S visited Section in morn.	
	20		Capt BLACKBURN. IN co-9-4 nurse will horse Ambulance proceeded to HURIONVILLE, to collect horses left by Division hurry through. returned in oft with one horse left by CFA in NOV 1916. ST HILAIRE etc	
	21		Capt BLACKBURN with detachment again proceeded to ST HILAIRE to collect horses left by Divisions	

WAR DIARY or INTELLIGENCE SUMMARY

Army Form C. 2118.

Place	Date	Hour	Summary of Events and Information	Remarks and references to Appendices
ECQUEDECQUES	FEBY 21 (cntd)		Detachment of 36 Mobile Vety Section proceeded to ST HILAIRE & collected 1 Horse from C.BTY. 160 Bde. 34 Division & returned to section in morn.	
	22		Inspection of 36 Mobile Veterinary Section by DDVS 1st Army & Portugese General. (General Joufelu), appliances Veterinary instruments etc. & expressed himself as very satisfied with Section.	
	23		21 Horses evacuated to No 18 VH from LILLERS i/c Sergt PLUMLEY & two men.	
	24		ADVS & DC (Col BLACKBURN) visited in car to ST HILAIRE reference horses collected on 20th	
	25		ADVS visited section in aft.	
	26		Return of conducting party from NEUFCHATEL. DDVS called in afternoon & gave instructions to OC 36 MVS reference collecting horses lost by PORTUGESE. DIVISION. in aft 1 NCO & 6 men proceeded to ST.HILAIRE & received 5 horses.	
	27		Report read in to DDVS. cart mare & horse collided. 5th Sergt PLUMLEY. H Temporary duty with 36 MVS transport to get Heavy Battery R.G.A. CANADIAN CORPS 1 Horse collided with AMBULANCE from ST.HILAIRE COTTES. ¶ Sergt APPLEBY. 36 MVS & 5 men proceeded to PORTUGESE DIVISION & loaded two horses received by 36 MVS & obtained receipt for same.	
	28		2 horses sold for slaughter to Buelan at LILLERS 190 fcs (for two) ADVS visited section in aft & examined sick horses & gave OC instructions reference MOVE.	

J Blackburn - Captn. AVC
OC.
36 Mobile Veterinary Section

Army Form C. 2118.

WAR DIARY or INTELLIGENCE SUMMARY
(Erase heading not required.)

Vol 19

Place	Date	Hour	Summary of Events and Information	Remarks and references to Appendices
ECQUEDECQUES	MARCH 1917 1		O.C. went to LABRUVIERE in aft. to ADVS.	
	2		Evacuated 12 horses for LILLERS to No 13 VH NEUFCHATEL. I/C of CH. v 1 man.	
	3		CAPTN LAURIE J.H. O.C. 36 MVS. returned from leave in morning relieving Capt BLACKBURN J. in temp ary command. ADVS pulled in aft. Capt ROGERS.E. went to NOEUX les MINES to take over new billet-	
	4		Section packing up preparatory to moving man off.	
	5		Section left ECGUEDECQUES in morn 7.50 & arrived after uneventful journey at NOEUXles MINES 12. Made very heavy & cut up most of the way.	
NOEUX les MINES	6		Section straightening up new billet. Medical Inspection in aft of 36 MVS. in event of reserving men for fighting units. 2 horses collected from FOUQUIERES 1 being floor case.	
	7		O.C. went to A.D.O.S. in morn. Walk afoot of Medical Inspection. Men of section paltering up at 9.15 floor pretty close down in washing, scaping skins from NOEUX les MINES.	
	8		Section facing up horse lines etc. for sick horses	
	9		28 horses evacuated to No 13 V.H. NEUFCHATEL I/C of Cpl & 2 men. O.C. went to BARLIN to A.D.V.S. in morn	
	10		No 2835 S.E. Pte BLAY.G.A. from No 1 Veterinary Hospital reported for duty to No 36 MVS.	
	11		A.D.V.S 3 United section in morn. Depo being paired for Advanced Collecting Post.	

Army Form C. 2118.

WAR DIARY
or
INTELLIGENCE SUMMARY.
(Erase heading not required.)

Instructions regarding War Diaries and Intelligence Summaries are contained in F. S. Regs., Part II. and the Staff Manual respectively. Title pages will be prepared in manuscript.

Place	Date	Hour	Summary of Events and Information	Remarks and references to Appendices
	MAR			
NOEUX les MINES	12		Gen NOBIN rode to PETIT SAINS & fixed up site for advanced billeting pat. at PETIT SAINS. Limber waggon carting mates for Retin billet stable etc. main coft. from NOEUX les MINES.	
	13		Limber waggon carting stone & manure for lines etc ADVSY DC to NOEUX les MINES pickingup surplus horses	
	14		Limber waggon carting etc.	
	15		A D V S visited in aft. the Pusphin hosp (10 cobs & 6 mules) brought into section Arms Inspection in afternoon	DAAQMG
	16		56 Horses wounded to No 13 VH NEUFCHATEL I/C of Sugt. 4 4 men. Col DOYLE visited section in afternoon.	
	17		Section facing up stalls for sick horses & strengthening wef raids of shed.	
	18		Lt Mullin went to BRUAY with two horses to be destroyed (for slaughter-house butchery)	
	19		Crew facing up stalls for sick horses (wind shields) morn & aft.	
	20		Men adjusting sick lines clothes & fitting up shelters am for breakwind.	
	21		ADVS visited in aft. received (6 mules) with horse sideing return from 21 Division	
	22		Rifle Inspection by DG to aft. Shoeing of fetlock knot. making breakwind with netting FRIDAY	
	23		55 Sick horses evacuated to No 13 Veterinary Hospital I/C of S/Sgt MILLER & 4 men.	
	24		Crew of section facing lines also for stable floor morn & aft.	
	25		O C visited in morning	

T.131. Wt. W708—776. 500000. 4/15. Sir J. C. & S.

Army Form C. 2118.

WAR DIARY
or
INTELLIGENCE SUMMARY.
(Erase heading not required.)

Place	Date	Hour	Summary of Events and Information	Remarks and references to Appendices
NOEUX les MINES	MARCH			
	26		Preparing Evacuation Rolls in afternoon. A.D.V.S. called in aft.	
	27		38 Sick horses evacuated to No 13 V.H. NEUFCHATEL. Lt. Rogers & 2 men, relief of conducting party for NEUFCHATEL.	
	28			
	29		Making up evacuation rolls in aft.	
	30		52 Horses 1st & 2nd Bn & 3 mew evacuated to No. 13 V.H. NEUFCHATEL	
	31			

Captn. AVC
OC.
36 Mobile Veterinary Sectn

24

Army Form C. 2118.

WAR DIARY
or
INTELLIGENCE SUMMARY.
(Erase heading not required.)

Vol 20

Instructions regarding War Diaries and Intelligence Summaries are contained in F.S. Regs., Part II. and the Staff Manual respectively. Title pages will be prepared in manuscript.

36th MOBILE VETERINARY SECTION
Date April 1917

Place	Date	Hour	Summary of Events and Information	Remarks and references to Appendices
NOEUX les MINES	APRIL			
	1		10 Horses evacuated ½ sick 1 MAN (in charge) from BETHUNE to No 23 Veterinary Hospital ST. OMER.	
	2		Anything up evacuating nulls in afternoon	
	3		Return of conducting parties from NEUFCHATEL & ST OMER. 51 Horses evacuated to NEUFCHATEL	
	4		In charge of 1 Sergt 4 men. 1 man with limber missed offer junction of ADVS from BARLIN to NOEUX les MINES	
	5		7 Horses evacuated by Barge from BETHUNE to No 23 V.H. ST OMER 1/c of 1 NCO.	
	6		A.B.W outfit in oft. Horse Ambulance returned 2 sick horses from Units moon agst.	
	7		36 horses evacuated to No 23 Veterinary Hospital ST OMER. 1/c of 1 NCO + 2 men Lpl MILLER returned from ST OMER.	
	8		Sgt BENTON & Party returned from NEUFCHATEL also Cpl ROGERS + conducting party 3 days.	
	9			
	10			
	11		16 horses evacuated by barge to ST OMER. 23 VH.	
	12		35 horses evacuated to No 23 VH ST OMER 1/c of Sergt 9 3 men. No 4067 Sgt BIRD.AE. from AFAB reported to 36 MVS for temporary duty. No 5455 Pte POWELL W.L. 36 MVS evacuated to No 1 CCS (Vesicular ?)	
	13		return of conducting party from ST OMER	
	14		return of conducting party from ST OMER.	

T.131. Wt. W708—776. 500000. 4/15. Sir J. C. & S.

Army Form C. 2118.

WAR DIARY
or
INTELLIGENCE SUMMARY.
(Erase heading not required.)

Instructions regarding War Diaries and Intelligence Summaries are contained in F.S. Regs., Part II. and the Staff Manual respectively. Title pages will be prepared in manuscript.

[Stamp: 36th MOBILE VETERINARY SECTION Date April 1917]

Place	Date	Hour	Summary of Events and Information	Remarks and references to Appendices
	April			
NOEUX les MINES	15		Started taking horses to Noeux les Mines but return being stilled returned with horses to Lillet	
MINES	16		40 Horses evacuated to No 23 V.H. STOMER from BETHUNE Station (on account of NOEUX les MINES station not being available on Railhead due to Shelling station	
	17		Return of conducting party from ST OMER	
	18		47 horses evacuated to No 23 V.H. STOMER i/c of B/Sgt & 4 men	
	19		Section packing up limber waggon etc. preparatory to moving	
	20		75 Horses evacuated to No 23 VH i/c of 1 Sergt & 5 men return of conducting party from ST OMER	
	21		Section packing up Limbers to moving	
	22		21 Horses evacuated to No 23 VH STOMER i/c 1 Cpl & 1 man	
FONTES	23		36 MVS left billet at NOEUX les MINES 8.15 a.m. arrived at billet FONTES after uneventful journey at 1.15 p.m. VIA BETHUNE CHOCQUES LILLERS. 7 Horses left behind (sick) will accompany section 1/1 North Midland Adv Veterinary Section AD Division abroad equipp'd & ADVS of arrival at FONTES	
MATRINGHEM	24		Section left FONTES les mon (9 a.m.) & proceeded to billet at MATRINGHEM arriving at 1.35 p.m. VIA WESTREHEM. LAIRES. DC proceeding with small party to MATRINGHEM & arranging billets for Section	
	25		Section busy fixing up horse lines, stables etc. man & afternoon. No 9795 Pte GEEWAVC 36 MVS evacuated to No 58 CCS	
	26		2 horses collected from BOMY in morning & 1 collected from LIETTRES in afternoon	

Army Form C. 2118.

WAR DIARY
or
INTELLIGENCE SUMMARY.
(Erase heading not required.)

Place	Date	Hour	Summary of Events and Information	Remarks and references to Appendices
	APRIL			
HATRINGHEM	26 Contd		No 18892 Pte SAMUEL J. from No 10 Veterinary Hospital NEUFCHATEL reported for duty with No 36 MVS.	
	27		2 Men hutting up sick lines etc	
	28		1 Horse collected from RENTY in morning	
	29		Several Lines sprayed in by which a worked with Calcium Sulphide	
	30		1 horse collected from WITTERNESSE with ambulance	

Signature
Captn. AVC
OC.
36 Mobile Veterinary Sectn

Army Form C. 2118.

WAR DIARY
or
INTELLIGENCE SUMMARY.
(Erase heading not required.)

Instructions regarding War Diaries and Intelligence Summaries are contained in F. S. Regs., Part II. and the Staff Manual respectively. Title pages will be prepared in manuscript.

Vol 21

26th MOBILE VETERINARY SECTION

Place	Date	Hour	Summary of Events and Information	Remarks and references to Appendices
MATRINGHEN	MAY 1		O.C. went to AIRE by horse, returned in evening.	
	2		Shoes of section horses clipped in morning.	
	3		Section paid in afternoon. ½ of Section marched to baths in afternoon.	
	4			
	5			
	6			
	7		7 horses evacuated to No 23 VH STOMER 1/c of 1 NCO	
	8		Off Mullin collected mails from BERGUENEUSE (16 DAC) Section packing up preparatory to leaving.	
NORRENT-FONTES	9		9 horses evacuated to ST.OMER. 1/c of NCO & 1 man. Section left MATRINGHEM. 6 AM. arrived billet at NORRENT-FONTES. 12.20 p.m. return of NCO from ST OMER.	
MORBECQUE	10		Section left NORRENT-FONTES for MORBECQUE arrived	
STEENVOORDE	11		Section left MORBECQUE 7 am arrived billet STEENVOORDE 12. via HAZEBROUCK.	
	12		Section left billet STEENVOORDE 5.30 a.m. arrived WINNEZEELE 9.45 a.m.	
WINNEZEELE	13		Section laid up horse etc. & prepared for next move.	
	14		Received advice of move on next day.	
	15		Section left WINNEZEELE at 7 a.m. arrived at POPERINGHE VIA STEENVOORDE, ABEELE.	

WAR DIARY or INTELLIGENCE SUMMARY.

36th MOBILE VETERINARY SECTION

Place	Date	Hour	Summary of Events and Information	Remarks and references to Appendices
POPERINGHE	MAY 15	9.15 a.m	Section busy with duties. Sick lines filling up. Have not having been except for a considerable time every duty in consequence at usual repairs. A.D.V.S. & 2 i/c Location in aft.	
	16		Section of conducting party from ST OMER after being in reinforcement camp 5 days	
	17		Section Busy with sick lines etc whole working unit valuable by pulling fresh crews on action. Paid in aft. A new free Divisional emblem ordered for temporary duty with MVS	
	18		No S.995 Pte BUCKLAND H AVC admitted for duty with 36 M VS from No 4 Veterinary Hospital.	
	19		Preparing evacuation roll. Working horse [hussars] & coal evacuation) with advanced outfield.	
	20		Lt Willis 41 men with 46 Horses proceeded by march to No 23 Veterinary Hospital ST OMER	
	21		O.D.V.S Bn Officer instructed NCO of service in use of new horse gas respirator.	
	22		Demonstration by Bn officer with new Fuller horse respirator. Officers i/c Bn of Various units in Division proceed also A.D.V.S. Practical demonstration given with Latin horses. 1 Horse evacuated to No 2 Mobile ST OMER by motor ambulance.	
	23		Return of conducting party from No 23 VH ST OMER. Demonstration given to Officers of Various Units with horse helmet (gas respirator)	
	24		Arm 9 respirator & Section Paid in aft. Supt BENTON 36 MVS proceeded with ADVS to DAC to give demonstration in use of gas respirators for horses.	

Army Form C. 2118.

WAR DIARY
or
INTELLIGENCE SUMMARY.
(Erase heading not required.)

Instructions regarding War Diaries and Intelligence Summaries are contained in F. S. Regs., Part II. and the Staff Manual respectively. Title pages will be prepared in manuscript.

Place	Date	Hour	Summary of Events and Information	Remarks and references to Appendices
POPERINGHE	MAY 1917 25		O.C. went to Watodo in morn re new billet out with voilage etc went to billet in aft. 1 man of section left I/c of new billet. O.C. reports ADVS office in aft.	
	26		Section at hird billet in aft. & provided with clean change of clothing	
	27		Sergt BENTON & 5 men proceeded by road with 27 horses to RYVELD (1st half) en route to no 25 V.H. ST OMER. Section packing waggons etc in aft.	
WESTOUTRE	28		36 MVS left billet & proceeded to new billet in RENINGHELST-ABEELE RD. arrived about 11. orderly despatched to HQ As advised HQ & DVS of location of Unit in afternoon. men of Section fixing up bivouacs etc & aid him in aft.	
	29		Fixed field lines erected in a country lane number of field horses arriving	
	30		Return of horsedealing party for road surrounding in aft.	
	31		Section found in afternoon. 1 NCO went with carts to DRC [?] collect dead cattle from farmers	

Signature
CAPTAIN A.V.C.
O.C. 36 MOBILE VETERINARY SECTION.

Army Form C. 2118.

WAR DIARY
or
INTELLIGENCE SUMMARY.
(Erase heading not required.)

Instructions regarding War Diaries and Intelligence Summaries are contained in F.S. Regs., Part II. and the Staff Manual respectively. Title pages will be prepared in manuscript.

36th M.O.R.U. VETERINARY SECTION — Date June 1917

Vol 22

Place	Date	Hour	Summary of Events and Information	Remarks and references to Appendices
WESTOUTRE	JUNE 1		4 men detailed to 6 MVS for temporary duty. Obtained batten Units. O.C. went to 6 MVS monthly conference.	with 36 M.V.S.
	2		O.C. and N.C.O. to men collecting post in morning. Evacuation orders made up in aft. No.14500 Pte HOLMWOOD J. AVC. returned for duty
	3		Cpl MILLER & 11 mounted men proceeded in road to STOMER with 66 horses daily sent to Batteries for exercise & part of exps.
	4		No 5019 Pte LEIPER J. AVC 36 MVS transferred to No 2 Veterinary Hospital HAVRE (being surplus)
	5		Ambulance Wagon with 10" wagon horn in aft for sick horse
	6		Return of conducting party NCO 11 men from evacuation to STOMER. In afternoon 1 NCO 1 man proceeded to Advanced collecting post on RENINGHELST VLAMERTINGHE Rd. Lumbar walk led etc also.
	7		O.C. went to X Corps MVS & made arrangements for evacuating by train. Evacuation will be made at Sickin paid in aft.
	8		44 horses taken to WIPPENHOEK siding to X Corps Mobile Veterinary Section. Two horses taken also in ambulance.
	9		1 NCO & four men proceeded to X Corps Mobile Veterinary Section for entraining horses. return of NCO & men and closing up of advanced collecting post.
	10		ADVS called in morning.
	11		6075 Pte CHARMER R. AVC. 36 MVS proceeded on leave to ENGLAND. O.C. went to X Corps Mobile Veterinary Detachment re-evacuating. Ann Inspection & practice with one Inspection in afternoon

Army Form C. 2118.

Instructions regarding War Diaries and Intelligence Summaries are contained in F. S. Regs., Part II. and the Staff Manual respectively. Title pages will be prepared in manuscript.

WAR DIARY
or
INTELLIGENCE SUMMARY.
(Erase heading not required.)

Place	Date	Hour	Summary of Events and Information	Remarks and references to Appendices
	JUNE			
WESTOUTRE	12.		12 horses taken to x corps Mobile Veterinary Detachment. Two cases later in ambulance.	
	13		19 men & 1 cart & 1 mule taken to x corps Mobile Veterinary Detachment for evacuation. C.C. went to HQ re new billet. & then looking up preparatory to departure.	
Nieukerke	14		Section packed up & departed from billet 2 p.m. arrived new billet about 4 p.m. fixed up each lines of Mobile Vet. section lints & shelters for men defaulted orderly to HQ and obtained Segraitis 9 a.D.V.S. of new location.	
	15		Men with cart with 13 horses taken to x corps Mobile Veterinary Detachment made enquiries for DDVS 2nd Army section putting up each line, latrine, incinerator, Area tent etc morning 4pt. section fixed up in afternoon.	
	16.		1 Sergt & 3 men proceeded to IX Corps Mobile Veterinary Detachment near BAILLEUL with 12 horses 2 horses taken to No 23 Veterinary Hospital in Motor Ambulance. Ambulance fitted two horse to Section in morning	
	17.		Invoid horses (shell wounds) brought in Section, fixing up troughs for horses	
	18		Putting up cookie each lines, owing to large number of horses coming in.	
	19		A.D.V.S. called in aft.	
	20		2 strayed horses brought to Section by MMP.	

T:134. Wt. W708-776. 500000. 4/15. Sir J.C.&S.

Army Form C. 2118.

Instructions regarding War Diaries and Intelligence Summaries are contained in F.S. Regs., Part II. and the Staff Manual respectively. Title pages will be prepared in manuscript.

WAR DIARY
or
INTELLIGENCE SUMMARY.
(Erase heading not required.)

[Stamp: 35th MOBILE VETERINARY SECTION Date June 30·19]

Place	Date	Hour	Summary of Events and Information	Remarks and references to Appendices
MAP 28 NIEUKERK	JUNE 21		Cpl ROGERS returned from temp. duty as clerk to A.D.V.S. (Blank in ENGLAND on 1 month leave.)	
	22		Sgt BENTON & party up to get destroy horses (road conducting). Evacuating cats made out ready for next day.	
	23			
	24		Cpl ROGERS & men proceed by road with 30 sick horses to No 23 Veterinary Hospital. Cpl MILLIER & party went to WIPPENHOEK asking with 35 sick horses for entraining two cases being taken by MOTOR AMBULANCE.	
	25		Sgt BENTON's party went WIPPENHOEK with 21 horses (mange) for entraining on 26th.	
	26		A NEUFCHATEL 1 NCO & 5 men train party. A D.V.S. called in aft. 1 horse destroyed. Hide removed.	
	27		Return of road conducting party in afternoon. 6 horses went to 1x Corps Mobile Veterinary Detachment in motor ambulance. 1 horse destroyed. Hide removed.	
	28		Return of Rail Conducting Party from NEUFCHATEL. ADVS left HQ in aft. for Rest Area.	
	29		Cpl ROGERS & 6 men conducted 45 horses to 1x Corps Mobile Veterinary Detachment near BAILLEUL.	
	30		Cpl MILLIER & 2 men conducted 5 horses to 1x Corps Mobile Veterinary Detachment. Overworked shortly removed to new Rest Area. had to bring own back again on account of horse. corpulin already there.	

[Signature]
CAPTAIN A.V.C.
O.C. 35 MOBILE VETERINARY SECTION.

Army Form C. 2118.

WAR DIARY
or
INTELLIGENCE SUMMARY.
(Erase heading not required.)

36th MOBILE VETERINARY SECTION
Date July 1917

Vol 22

Instructions regarding War Diaries and Intelligence Summaries are contained in F. S. Regs., Part II. and the Staff Manual respectively. Title pages will be prepared in manuscript.

Place	Date	Hour	Summary of Events and Information	Remarks and references to Appendices
N/central forward area	July 1st		O.C. went to H.Q. reference moving orders.	
		2nd	O.C. went in car to select billets for section.	
		3	Section packing up ready for moving on next day evacuation roll made up of animals left in charge of incoming 35 MVS 27 Division	
PRADELLES		4	36 MVS left N/central 7 a.m. via LOCRE BAILLEUL STRAZEELE arriving at billet in PRADELLES early in afternoon.	
LA BELLE CROIX		5	36 MVS left PRADELLES 7.15 a.m. for billet at LA BELLE CROIX, NA RACQUINGHEM in afternoon. Section forming up Divisional trek with horses, silently departed to Signal office at ST OMER Advisory Off. Lynnie of O/C 36 MVS of location of unit	
		6	Section forming up billet de manu & afternoon	
		7	Rifle & Bec Repair in de inspection in afternoon. Ambulance (horse) repaired at local wheelwrights	
		8	O.C. wants D.A.L. & inspects horses.	
		9	O.C. inspects horses of 1914 log at 5 in morning	
		10	No. 2157 Sergt ELLIOTT A.E. A.V.C. reported to O.C 36 Mobile Veterinary Section for duty from No. 9 Veterinary Hospital.	
		11	O.C. inspects D.A.L. horses	

T.1134. Wt. W708—776. 500000. 4/15. Sir J. C. & S.

Army Form C. 2118.

WAR DIARY
or
INTELLIGENCE SUMMARY.
(Erase heading not required.)

56th MOBILE VETERINARY SECTION
Date July 1917

Place	Date	Hour	Summary of Events and Information	Remarks and references to Appendices
	JULY			
LA BELLE CROIX	12		Section pushing out preparations to leaving next day.	
PRADELLES	13		Section left LA BELLE CROIX in morn 7.30 arrived at PRADELLES about 12.30 via HAZEBROUCK	
			CM MILLIER NCO man went to No 23 Veterinary Hospital ST OMER with sick horses & joined Section later in day at PRADELLES.	
	14		36 MVS left PRADELLES in morn 7am VIA BAILLEUL-LOCRE and arrived at billet MC central 12.30.	
			Horses fixed up for picketing - sick Horses. Ambulance Links to orderly dropped within to RA. Hdqts & messages sent by DRLS to 24 Div Hdqts to 9 Squadn. 2 AD VS	
M C central Sheet 28	15		O.C. went to No 20 x 1 mobile horses, also to 23 Durerian MVS.	
	16		O.C. inspected horses of D.A.C. 16 horses taken to Wittenbroek sidings. 1/c of NCO & 3 men proceeding to NO 13 Y H	
			NEUFCHATEL with horses. 1/c of NCO & Detachment.	
	17		3 men returned from & bomb Mobile detachment in evening. Ambulance taken to 194 boy for repair left	
	18		O.C. inspected horses of D.A.C.	
	19		Men of Section paid in aft. Box respirator drill also in aft. O.C. inspected horses DAC	
	20		O.C. Inspected horses D.A.C.	
	21		NO 455 PTE EAGLE J. AVC 36 MVS returned from leave (reinforcement camp in aft). O.C. inspected horses of D.A.C.	
	22		11 horses taken to 11 Corps Mobile Veterinary detachment in afternoon Section packing up preparatory to leaving next day.	

Army Form C. 2118.

WAR DIARY
or
INTELLIGENCE SUMMARY.
(Erase heading not required.)

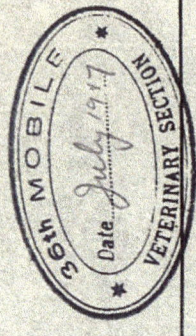

Place	Date	Hour	Summary of Events and Information	Remarks and references to Appendices
MLL33	JULY 23.		Lectun moved into new billet. fracing up sick linin etc in afternoon	
	24		Sergt ELLIOTT + 3 men went to II corps Mobile Veterinary Detachment to form of Section.	
	25		36 horses evacuated to II corps Mobile Veterinary Detachment	
	26		Float collected 1 horse	
	27		Lectun fund in afternoon. advanced collecting post established up near DICKEBUSCH in aft Sergt BENTON + 1 man proceeded to new post in evening	
	28		Float collected 3 horses during day. PTE REYNOLDS. M.A.V.C. 36 M.V.S. proceeded to ENGLAND on leave.	
	29			
	30		36 horses evacuated by road to NO 2 3V.H. STOMER in morning 1/c of off + 6 men.	

Signature

CAPTAIN A.V.C.
O.C. 36 MOBILE VETERINARY SECTION.

Army Form C. 2118.

Instructions regarding War Diaries and Intelligence Summaries are contained in F.S. Regs, Part II. and the Staff Manual respectively. Title pages will be prepared in manuscript.

WAR DIARY or INTELLIGENCE SUMMARY.

(Erase heading not required.)

36th MOBILE VETERINARY SECTION
Date 1 Aug 1917

Vol 24

Place	Date	Hour	Summary of Events and Information	Remarks and references to Appendices
MT 32 In the field	Aug 1		20 horses Evacuated to II Corps MVD & 1 float case in ambulance 1/c of 6/s & 3 men	
	2		11 mules taken in cart to II Corps MVD in morning return party from road constructing 23 V.H. STOMER	
	3		SADVS visited Section & advanced Billetting post.	
	4		Advanced Collecting post abandoned & NCO & men returned to Section. Section paid in afternoon.	
	5		47 horses Evacuated to II Corps MVD. Road cases & their cases also cart with forage.	
	6			
	7		DDVS visited Section in morning & Inspected DAC horse smoke. cart with breed when they arise went to II Corps Mobile Veterinary Detachment. Evacuation rolls made out in aft.	
	8		Sgt Beinten & 6 men proceeded by road with 36 horses to No 23 Veterinary Hospital STOMER.	
	9		Pte REYNOLDS returned from leave. Evacuation rolls made out in aft.	
	10		Sergt APPLEBY & men went with 20 horses (lame cases) & 1 float case to II Corps MVD.	
	11		6.l inspection removerd DAC in afternoon.	
	12			
	13		Cpl MILLIER & men proceeded by road with 42 horses to No 23 Veterinary Hospital STOMER. Float used with 1 case to II Corps MVD in afternoon.	

Army Form C. 2118.

WAR DIARY
or
INTELLIGENCE SUMMARY.
(Erase heading not required.)

Instructions regarding War Diaries and Intelligence Summaries are contained in F. S. Regs., Part II. and the Staff Manual respectively. Title pages will be prepared in manuscript.

35th MOBILE VETERINARY SECTION

Place	Date	Hour	Summary of Events and Information	Remarks and references to Appendices
In the Field	Aug 14		S.Sgt APPLEBY & 4 men proceeded to II Corps Mobile Veterinary Detachment I/c of 32 Horses (Train cases) ADVS II Corps visited Section in aft.	
	15		Return of conducting party from STOMER. Section paid in afternoon.	
	16		ADVS II Corps visited Section in morn.	
	17		S.Sgt APPLEBY & 3 men proceeded to II Corps MVD with 14 horses (train cases)	
	18		L/Cpl ROGERS & 9 men proceeded to No 23 Veterinary Hospital with 54 horses (Road evacuation)	
	19		1 Road case brought in by Ambulance in morning.	
	20			
	21		24 Train cases & 12 Road cases taken to II Corps MVD I/c of NCO & 4 men also out milk forage.	
	22		No 500 Pte UPTON proceeded on leave. 24 Train cases & 12 Road cases taken to II Corps MVD in afternoon.	
	23		Section paid in aft.	
	24		Sick horses mustered & Mobile Section horses also in afternoon	
	25		Sgt BENTON proceeded to No 22 VH STOMER with 60 sick horses	
	26		Issue of Road bikes to II Corps MVD	
	27		Ambulance made two trips to II Corps Mobile Veterinary Detachment	

Return of No 1333 2 SS WESTLEY from leave

1577 Wt. W10791/1773 500,000 1/15 D. D. & L. A.D.S.S./Forms/C. 2118.

Army Form C. 2118.

WAR DIARY
or
INTELLIGENCE SUMMARY.
(Erase heading not required.)

Instructions regarding War Diaries and Intelligence Summaries are contained in F. S. Regs., Part II. and the Staff Manual respectively. Title pages will be prepared in manuscript.

Place	Date	Hour	Summary of Events and Information	Remarks and references to Appendices
In the Field	AUG 28		O/C MILLIER proceeded with 36 sick horses for No 23 V.H. STOMER. S.Sergt APPLEBY & Conducting party proceeded with 32 sick horses to II Corps Mobile Veterinary Detachment. Also 2 ambulance cases for II Corps M.V.D. return of conducting party from STOMER.	
	29		5 Train Buses & 3 Road Buses taken to II Corps M.V.D. in afternoon	
	30		12 Train Buses taken to II Corps M.V.D. Return of detachment 1 Sergt + 4 men from II Corps M.V.D.	
	30		Section paid in afternoon	
	31		Pte HALL 3 36 MVS proceeds for train duty to & from advanced veterinary Post.	

B. S. [signature]
CAPTAIN A.V.C.
O.C. 36 MOBILE VETERINARY SECTION.

Army Form C. 2118.

WAR DIARY
or
INTELLIGENCE SUMMARY
(Erase heading not required.)

36th M.V.S.

Vol 25

Army Form C. 2118.

WAR DIARY
or
INTELLIGENCE SUMMARY.
(Erase heading not required.)

Instructions regarding War Diaries and Intelligence Summaries are contained in F. S. Regs., Part II. and the Staff Manual respectively. Title pages will be prepared in manuscript.

[Stamp: 26th MOBILE VETERINARY SECTION September 1917]

Place	Date	Hour	Summary of Events and Information	Remarks and references to Appendices
In the Field	SEPTEMBER			
	1		40 Horses evacuated to IX Corps M.V.D	
	2		Sergt ELLIOTT & 5 men proceeded to No 23 V.H. ST OMER with 32 horses	
	3		NCOs & men of Section holding views that for men "mending dug outs against bombs etc. Section waggon painted in afternoon. & repairing stable floors.	
	4		Section waggon painted in afternoon. & repairing stable floors.	
	5		Return of Bombarding party in apt from ST OMER	
	6		1 Horse brought in by ambulance in morning Section paid in afternoon	
	7		Section waggon painted.	
	8		34 Horses evacuated to 1st Australian Veterinary Detachment	
	9		77 Horses evacuated by road to 23 Veterinary Hospital ST OMER. I/c of NCOs & 14 men (with 7 R.F.A. half for evacuating)	
	10		Waggons overhauled & painted & walk hung faced ready for moving.	
	11		Waggon. stable loading gear packed in morning	
	12		Return of conducting party from ST OMER section packing waggons etc.	
	13		NCO sent in advance to STEENVOORDE to secure billet Sergt ELLIOTT proceeded with sick horses to 1st Australian Veterinary Casualty Clearing Station & Sergt BENTON went with Dismounties case to 10 Corps M.V.D	
	14		Section left billet for STEENVOORDE 4.30 arrived at billet 11.30. A/Lyte Q.M. Punch. & DADVS advised of new location	

WAR DIARY
or
INTELLIGENCE SUMMARY.

Army Form C. 2118.

Place	Date	Hour	Summary of Events and Information	Remarks and references to Appendices
In the Field	SEPT 15		Section packing up preparatory to moving to new Sector.	
	16		Section left billet 4.30 arrival at Station 6 did not entrain till 2 next morning	
	17		Arrival at BAPAUME STATION 12.30 proceeded to new billet. fixed up tents lech lines etc advised O. officer signals & DADVS of new location	
	18		Pte BUCKLAND to proceeded on leave to ENGLAND	
	19		O.C. proceeded to new billet at LEMESNIL in aft. section packing up preparatory to leaving	
	20		Section left billet at N.11.A.5.7 4.30 and arrival at billet LEMESNIL 10.15 advised O.C. "Signals".	
	21		DADVS of new location. Orderly proceeded to ADVS & Corps with return & advice of new location Section busy making lines & standings for horses. ADVS & Corps visited section in evening. Section find it difficult to find fir standing O.C. went to C.R.E. & the Corps re materials for erecting stabling. section fixing up found fir stabling	
	22		Section putting in posts for stabling etc	
	23		DADVS visited Section in afternoon Section erecting work stabling	
	24		O.C. rode to Div Hqtrs in morning. Pte LOTT returned from leave. Section busy erecting stabling	
	25		Section busy erecting stabling	
	26		Section packing up preparatory to leaving next day. Section fixed in aft	
	27		Section left LE MESNIL in morn S and Corps ROGERS went-on in advance to PERONNE to obtain billets through Town Major Section arrived PERONNE 11.45. Signals & DADVS advised of location of section	

Army Form C. 2118.

WAR DIARY
or
INTELLIGENCE SUMMARY.

(Erase heading not required.)

Instructions regarding War Diaries and Intelligence Summaries are contained in F. S. Regs., Part II. and the Staff Manual respectively. Title pages will be prepared in manuscript.

36th MOBILE VETERINARY SECTION
Date Sept. 30 1917

Place	Date	Hour	Summary of Events and Information	Remarks and references to Appendices
In the Field	Sept 28		Section left billet at PERONNE & arrived at billet "VRAIGNES" taking over from 4th MVS.	
	29		In aft action facing up lines billets etc. Dris Hill & Squires & DADVS acknowed of location of Unit. Section busy with stable floors curtains hurdles for oven. DADVS called here O.C. in afternoon	
	30		O.C. went to Dri Hughes in morn. Section busy with stable floors etc.	

W. J. [signature]
CAPTAIN A.V.C.
O.C. 36 MOBILE VETERINARY SECTION.

T.131. Wt. W703-776. 500000. 4/15. Sir J. C. & S.

Confidential

Vol 26

War Diary
of
36 Mobile Veterinary
Section

1st October 1917.

Army Form C. 2118.

WAR DIARY
or
INTELLIGENCE SUMMARY.
(Erase heading not required.)

Instructions regarding War Diaries and Intelligence Summaries are contained in F. S. Regs., Part II. and the Staff Manual respectively. Title pages will be prepared in manuscript.

36th MOBILE VETERINARY SECTION

Place	Date	Hour	Summary of Events and Information	Remarks and references to Appendices
In the Field	Oct			
	1		Section busy cutting birchen briths & refining stable flooring.	
	2		Section refining stable flooring, fencing out front & water trough. DADVS called in aft.	
	3		No 8849 Pte BUCKLAND H returned from leave.	
	4		Visit by ADVS III Corps & DDVS III Army to Section & inspected Horse Billets etc.	
	5		Evacuating Rolls made out in afternoon. 5926 Sery BENTON proceeded on leave.	
	6		No 1694 Pte SAMUEL J. returned from leave. Pte MILLIER 4.5 now proceeded by train with 44 Sick horses to No 7 Veterinary Hospital FORGES les EAUX. No 1592 Pte SAMUEL J AVC returned from leave.	
	7		No 735456 DR IMPEY proceeded on leave.	
	8		06 infected horses of BAC. in morn. & return of conducting party from FORGES les EAUX.	
	9		Section making standings for horses in Sick line Stable.	
	10		New ambulance brought from ROISEL Stn in morn & old one taken down as STN. DADVS left division for 5 Vety Hospital ABBEVILLE Major LEANING	
	11		Section paid in aft. No 5051 Pte WRIGHT. J AVC SGMVS proceeded to ENGLAND on leave. No 3512	
	12		Visit from new DADVS 24 Div in aft. Had went for Sick horse in morning. Pte HALL G AVC proceeded on leave ENGLAND.	
	13		Pte MILLIER with 4.5 horses & party proceeded to FORGES-les-EAUX. ROISEL Station. American General & Col DOYLE inspected Section.	
	14		ADVS III Corps visited Section in aft. Pte ROGERS No 12663 proceeded on leave.	
	15		Return of Conducting party from FORGES les EAUX. No 7 Veterinary Hospital. new refining roofs of stable stables.	

1577 Wt.W10791/1773 500,000 1/15 D.D.&L. A.D.S.S./Forms/C. 2118.

Army Form C. 2118.

WAR DIARY
or
INTELLIGENCE SUMMARY.
(Erase heading not required.)

Instructions regarding War Diaries and Intelligence Summaries are contained in F. S. Regs., Part II. and the Staff Manual respectively. Title pages will be prepared in manuscript.

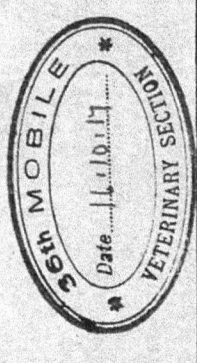

Place	Date	Hour	Summary of Events and Information	Remarks and references to Appendices
Lull	Oct 16		Section busy repairing stable floors & roofs.	
	17		Returns taken by O C to DADVS in morning. Ambulance collected sick horse in afternoon.	
	18		Waggon went to MVD brought back body shot use of timber for stables. No 5986 Sgt BENTON W. ave. returned from leave. New of Section paid in afternoon.	
	19		Section fitting up hand pump in sheds of P.H. Stove.	
	20		1 Sgt & 3 men proceeded by tram to No 7 VH FORGES les EAUX with 31 sick animals.	
	21		O C 24 Division in hotel billet, horses, etc., in morning.	
	22		Section fixing up stable funnels.	
	23		S/Sgt APPLEBY C/Sgt. for ENGLAND: 24.10.17 — 4.11.17 leave.	
	24		DADVS visited Section in morn. Section now facing standings trod for vehicles, repairing roof.	
			Pte JEFFREY F.R.V.C. proceed to ENGLAND on leave 25.10.17 — 5.11.17.	
	25		Section busy repairing stable floors & fixing up brick standings for vehicles.	
	26		Visit by ADVS 7 Corps & DADVS 24 Division. Stables buildings & mess huts inspected, orderly despatched to H Lance MVS & arrangements made with O C for Evacuation of Mange.	
	27		Cpl & 2 men proceeded by tram with 15 sick animals to No 7 VH FORGES-EAUX. No 5081 Pte WRIGHT J. ave & No 14500 Pte HOLMWOOD J. returned from leave.	

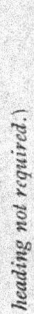

Army Form C. 2118.

WAR DIARY
or
INTELLIGENCE SUMMARY.
(Erase heading not required.)

Instructions regarding War Diaries and Intelligence Summaries are contained in F. S. Regs., Part II. and the Staff Manual respectively. Title pages will be prepared in manuscript.

Place	Date	Hour	Summary of Events and Information	Remarks and references to Appendices
VRAIGNES	Oct 28		The Section was inspected by the D.V.S., D.D.V.S. Army, & A.D.V.S. Corps.	
	29		We have made a number of Canvas Water Carriers for holding water for horses en route to Hospital. These buckets are made after the style of the water carriers used by natives in India, and hold about eight gallons. The material used is strong waterproof Canvas, a coat of paint being added on the outside to prevent any possibility of leaking. The buckets are made with a large round bottom so that when filled they will stand upright. The neck is about three & a half inches in diameter and is provided with a strong piece of cord so that it can be tied across to prevent loss of water in the wind. The carrier being secured over by rough shouldering etc. These buckets will form part of the equipment of the collecting posts and will be brought back by them on their return to M.V.S.	
	30		L/Cpl Rogers, Pre Hall & Pre Bloy returned from leave. No 21544 Pte Reynolds M. admitted to hospital. Up to the present time 5,210 horses have passed through this Section since the date of codisembarking in France.	
	31			

B. ?. Capt A.V.C.
1/c 36 Mobile Vety Section

VM 27

Secret

War Diary.
36th Mobile Veterinary Section.
from Nov 1st to Nov 30th
1917.

Army Form C. 2118.

WAR DIARY
or
INTELLIGENCE SUMMARY.
(Erase heading not required.)

Place	Date	Hour	Summary of Events and Information	Remarks and references to Appendices
VRAIGNES	Nov 2		Capt W.A. MACGREGOR AVC YOM² 24th Divisional Train arrived for temporary duty with this Section during the absence of Capt J.H. LAURIE AVC on leave.	
	3. 20		During this period all have been very busy dressing animals sent to this section with Sarcoptic Mange. All animals sent in were thoroughly examined and in some cases parasites were found, these were evacuated to Base Veterinary Hospital for further treatment. The cases in which no parasite could be found were washed and dressed with Calcium Sulphide and kept in isolation for a period of two to three days when they were returned to their respective units.	
	14		One canvas water carrier reported to in War Diary 1st October was dispatched to A.D.V.S. 55th Division for the use of 1/1 W. Lancs Mobile Veterinary Section. The Section was inspected by the Chief of the French Veterinary Staff of the neighbouring French Division accompanied by D.A.D.V.S. 24th Division	
	15		Capt. J.H. LAURIE AVC returned from leave. Under orders received from A.D.V.S. VII Corps through D.A.D.V.S. 24th Division, two men were dispatched to VII Corps Mobile Veterinary Detachment temporarily located at VILLERS FAUCON during	

1577 Wt. W10791/1773 500,000 1/15 D. D. & L.   A.D.S.S./Forms/C. 2118.

Army Form C. 2118.

WAR DIARY
or
INTELLIGENCE SUMMARY.
(Erase heading not required.)

Instructions regarding War Diaries and Intelligence Summaries are contained in F. S. Regs., Part II. and the Staff Manual respectively. Title pages will be prepared in manuscript.

Place	Date	Hour	Summary of Events and Information	Remarks and references to Appendices
VRAIGNES	20 & 20-30		The forward junction for temporary duty. During this period we have had trying the places our horses fill as a protection against picking up nails, but up to the present it has been found that in one or two cases the plates have broken off. A full report will be rendered to D.A.D.V.S. 24th Division on this subject by 10th December. A.D.V.S. VII Corps visited the sections and inspected one or two animals that had got the plates under the shoes.	

J. W. Lamm Capt a V C

1577 Wt.W10791/1773 500,000 1/15 D. D. & L. A.D.S.S./Forms/C. 2118.

Confidential.

36 Mobile Veterinary Section.
War Diary
December 1917.

Army Form C. 2118.

WAR DIARY
or
INTELLIGENCE SUMMARY.
(Erase heading not required.)

Instructions regarding War Diaries and Intelligence Summaries are contained in F. S. Regs., Part II. and the Staff Manual respectively. Title pages will be prepared in manuscript.

Place	Date	Hour	Summary of Events and Information	Remarks and references to Appendices
VRAIGNES	DECEMBER			
	1		During this period the Rex plates for horses fur nova as a preventative against	
	2		horses picking up nails were tried on some of the Auton-horses and it was	
	3		found that in most instances the plates broke, or became flat. It was also	
	4		found that they were liable to cause Thrush.	
	5		A full report on this subject was rendered to D.A.D.V.S. 2nd Division	
	10		on the 10th inst.	
	12		D.D.V.S. Cavalry Corps and A.D.V.S. 5th Cavalry Division inspected the Section billets.	
	13-28		O.C. took over the temporary duties of D.A.D.V.S. during the absence of the D.A.D.Y.S. on leave to England.	
	26		O.C. took over the Veterinary charge of 76 Brigade R.G.A. under instructions received from D.D.V.S. Cavalry Corps. It was found necessary to evacuate 19 animals of this Brigade for Mange, and every hour been undertaken to keep this steam disease as low as possible. It is not thought advisable to clip their animals owing to the cold weather.	
	29		D.D.V.S. Cavalry Corps visited this Section and afterwards proceeded	

Army Form C. 2118.

WAR DIARY
or
INTELLIGENCE SUMMARY.
(Erase heading not required.)

Instructions regarding War Diaries and Intelligence Summaries are contained in F.S. Regs., Part II. and the Staff Manual respectively. Title pages will be prepared in manuscript.

Place	Date	Hour	Summary of Events and Information	Remarks and references to Appendices
VRAIGNES	DECEMBER 29		Wrote O.C. to inspect the 76 Brigade R.G.A. D.D.R. Cavalry Corps and D.A.D.V.S. 24th Division raised this section for the purpose of inspecting sick animals for casting.	
	30		During the month this Section has evacuated 176 animals, making a total of 5567 since this Section came overseas in 1915. In order to reduce the amount of animal wastage, 14 animals have been treated in this Section and returned to duty during the month of December.	

J. S. ----
Capt. A.V.C.
O.C. 36 Mobile Veterinary Section

Confidential

36 Mobile Veterinary Section
War Diary
for the month of
January 1918.

Army Form C. 2118.

WAR DIARY
or
INTELLIGENCE SUMMARY.
(Erase heading not required.)

Instructions regarding War Diaries and Intelligence Summaries are contained in F. S. Regs., Part II. and the Staff Manual respectively. Title pages will be prepared in manuscript.

Place	Date	Hour	Summary of Events and Information	Remarks and references to Appendices
VRAIGNES	1		OC inspected all horses of 76 Brigade R.F.A. D.A.D.V.S. 24 Division visited this Section and inspected animals for evacuation to Base.	
	2		N.C.Os and men were inspected by Medical Officer for scabies. OC raised 33 Labour Co.	
	3		Visited the 24 D.A.C. and examined all animals for Contagious Disease.	
	4		Visited the 76 Brigade R.F.A. and arrangements were made for some of the horses suffering from skin disease to be treated with Calcium Sulphide, pending the opening of the Horse Dep at BEAUMETZ.	
	5		A.D.V.S. 5 Cavalry Division visited this Section, and made arrangements with OC to visit 76 Brigade R.F.A. on 6th inst.	
	6		OC visited 76 Brigade R.F.A. with A.D.V.S. 5th Cavalry Division. Horses suffering with skin disease were sent to this Section for evacuation to Base.	
	7		Visited the 33rd Labour Co. and 24 D.A.C.	
	8		Box Respirators and P.H. Helmets of the N.C.Os and men of this Section were inspected and found in good order.	
	9		D.A.D.V.S 24 Division visited this Section and inspected all animals for evacuation to Base.	
	10		Six animals sent to this Section suffering with suspected Mange were	

A 5534 Wt. W4973/M687 750,000 8/16 D. D. & L. Ltd. Forms/C.2118/13.

WAR DIARY or INTELLIGENCE SUMMARY

Army Form C. 2118.

Place	Date	Hour	Summary of Events and Information	Remarks and references to Appendices
	10		put through the Horse Dip at BEAUMETZ.	
	11		All animals of 113 Heavy Battery R.G.A. 76 Brigade were also put through the Dip.	
	12		A specimen Water Cart was made by the Section who are running disinfector to Base was proceeded to the South. Of Veterinary Service for inspection.	
	13		All animals of 132 Heavy Battery R.G.A. 9 Brigade R.H. and to the Horse Dip.	
	14-22		During this period 120 Section were busy thoroughly House standings etc in order to provide for all cases of Ophthalmia to be treated in the Section.	
	23		All animals of No 2 Section 24 D.A.C. were sent to the Horse Dip at BEAUMETZ.	
	24-31		During this period the Section has been very busy with the treatment of Ophthalmia cases, no fewer than 64 cases being treated with Lysols solution during the period. 15 cases have been cured and 12 animals returned to duty, the remainder are still in the Section for further treatment. Cases that show no signs of improvement will be evacuated to Base. Horse cases of suspected Mange were put through the Horse Dip at BEAUMETZ. N.C.O's and men were billeted ready scanned for Scabies.	

F.R.Kamm Capt AVC.

Confidential

36 Mobile Veterinary Section

War Diary for the month of

February 1918.

WAR DIARY
or
INTELLIGENCE SUMMARY.
(Erase heading not required.)

Army Form C. 2118.

Place	Date	Hour	Summary of Events and Information	Remarks and references to Appendices
VRAIGNES	July 1		Five animals affected with skin disease were sent through the Horse Depot at Boves Brainville, and 5 mangeyness made to the depot of chow animals with skin disease.	
	2		N.C.O's and men were medically examined for scabies.	
	3		O.C. round 76th Brigade R.G.A. and pickets out animals suffering from skin disease which were evacuated to Base.	
	4		D.A.D.V.S. 2nd Division visited the lines and examined all animals for evacuation to Base.	
	5		All animals of 113 Hy. Bty R.G.A. passed through the Horse Depot at Boves, and 3 that had been admitted to the Action for treatment.	
	6		O.C. visited 132 Hy Bty R.G.A. and examined all animals for Contagious Diseases. Three officers and 3 men sickness and injury were sent to this Action for evacuation to Base.	
	7		D.A.D.V.S. 2nd Division visited the Action and examined all animals for evacuation to Base.	

Army Form C. 2118.

WAR DIARY
or
INTELLIGENCE SUMMARY.
(Erase heading not required.)

Instructions regarding War Diaries and Intelligence Summaries are contained in F. S. Regs., Part II. and the Staff Manual respectively. Title pages will be prepared in manuscript.

Place	Date	Hour	Summary of Events and Information	Remarks and references to Appendices
VIGNEUX	8-16		N.C.O's and men of the section were instructed in the use of the rifle, loading, firing the Rifle. Men had also been carrying out drill on foot. O.C. H.K and Veterinary charge of 187 Labour Coy at FLECHIN.	
	17		O.C. visited 24th D.A.E. and examined all animals of Can in Reserve.	
	18		Being in the presence of Mangemon 113 Hy Bty R.G.A. O.C. Section visited	
	19		the battery and vicinity and made arrangements for evacuation of sick horses	
	20		the horse lines keeping stabled. D.A.D.V.S. 24 Division also visited these lines with	
	21		O.C. and inspected all animals.	
	22		132 H Bty R.G.A. transferred to 3 Cavalry Division. H.Q.H.Q.R.A 200 Brigade	
	17		H.Q. H. Bde 3 Cavalry Division.	
	23-27		No change, inspection of troops of Artillery & of horses picketing, sheep for O.C. C. Bornwood and also of the pic aduros afour sup for the lymphangitis have been reviewed, an adverse report of A.Co was made and sent to VILLERS BRETONNEUX for veterinary purposes. The Division being unfortunate to have met with bad weather	
	28		One section received from D.A.D.V.S. re-called as reserve being	

J. K. [signature]
Capt a V.C.
O.C. 36 Mob Veterinary Section

Confidential

36 Mobile Veterinary Section
    24 Division

War Diary

For the month of

March 1918.

Army Form C. 2118.

WAR DIARY
or
INTELLIGENCE SUMMARY.
(Erase heading not required.)

Instructions regarding War Diaries and Intelligence Summaries are contained in F. S. Regs., Part II. and the Staff Manual respectively. Title pages will be prepared in manuscript.

Place	Date	Hour	Summary of Events and Information	Remarks and references to Appendices
VRAIGNES	March 1		Section busy repairing stables site D.A.D.V.S visited the Section in the morning and examined animals for evacuation	
	2		N.C.O's men were medically examined for scabies	
	3		Section busy packing up from to a move. 1/2 B. Laws M.V.S. arrived & took new billet	
BOUVINCOURT	4		Section left Vraignes for BOUVINCOURT.	
	5		D.A.D.V.S 3d Division visited the Section and inspected the billet	
	6		Stables were repaired and thoroughly cleaned up.	
	7		D.A.D.V.S visited the Section and examined animals for evacuation	
	8		23 animals were evacuated to No.7 Veterinary Hospital.	
	9		A.D.V.S. XIX Corps visited the Section and inspected the billet	
	10		Camp Commandant XIX Corps visited the Section	
	11		3 cases of Mobilation were admitted & 4 men before being evacuated	
	12		Orders were received to move to TERTRY	
	13		Section moved from BOUVINCOURT to TERTRY	
TERTRY	14		N.C.O's & men on fatigues cleaning up the billet and repairing	
	15		stables, mess room, kitchen, recreation Guard Room etc.	

Army Form C. 2118.

WAR DIARY
or
INTELLIGENCE SUMMARY.
(Erase heading not required.)

Instructions regarding War Diaries and Intelligence Summaries are contained in F. S. Regs., Part II. and the Staff Manual respectively. Title pages will be prepared in manuscript.

Place	Date	Hour	Summary of Events and Information	Remarks and references to Appendices
TERTRY	16-21		Action still in progress, cleaning up etc. 3 A.D.V.S. 2nd Division training	
			Action and removed arrivals for training "March" other training	
	22		Action left TERTRY for BRIE. 2.15 p.m left BRIE for VILLERS CARBONNEL.	
	23		6.20 am moved from VILLERS CARBONNEL to LIHONS. 9.30 pm left LIHONS	
	24		for HARBONNIERES.	
HARBONNIERES	25		Division left HARBONNIERES and arrived at TAINNES. 16 horse evacuated from BOVES STN.	
	26		Action still mar "March 16" orders.	
TAINNES	27		Left BOVES and TAINNES and arrived at BOVES. 8 horse evacuated from SALLY STATION	
	28		Move from BOVES to COTTENCHY.	
COTTENCHY	29	4 AM	Orders were received to proceed to NAMPTY, and arrived there at 10.15 a.m	
	30		Action left NAMPTY for BUYON.	
BUYON	31		During the last 10 days the division has been continually on the move, and sick animals, mostly wounded, have been evacuated whilst on the "line of march".	

[signature] Captain R.V.C.

Confidential

War Diary

For the month
of
April 1918.

36 Mobile Veterinary Section.

WAR DIARY or INTELLIGENCE SUMMARY

Army Form C. 2118.

Place	Date	Hour	Summary of Events and Information	Remarks and references to Appendices
BUYON	1.4.18		O.C. visited 24 Divisional Train and inspected all animals for Contagious Diseases.	
	2.4.18		D.A.D.V.S. 24 Division visited the Section this morning and examined all animals before they were evacuated to Base.	
	3		5 cases of Mule Wounds were received by this Section during the morning, all of which were treated before being evacuated to Base in the afternoon.	
	4		Orders were received for this Section to move to VERS at 8 a.m.	
VERS	5		Section busy cleaning up ready for the line of march in the morning.	
	6		Section left VERS for PETIT CAGNY, arrived at PETIT CAGNY at 3.30 p.m.	
PETIT CAGNY	7.		A.D.V.S. XIX Corps visited the Section in the morning. 11 p.m. Orders were received to proceed to CLAIRY in the morning.	
CLAIRY.	8		Arrived at CLAIRY 4.45 p.m. Instructions were received from C.R.A. to an advanced party to meet the Staff Captain R.A. at ANDAINVILLE Church at 12 noon on 9th inst. Advance party were detailed to meet the Staff Captain. Section left CLAIRY for ANDAINVILLE.	
ANDAINVILLE	10		O.C. visited 106, 107 Bde R.F.A. + 24th D.A.C. and arranged for all sick animals to be sent to this Section for examination to Base.	

Army Form C. 2118.

WAR DIARY
or
INTELLIGENCE SUMMARY.
(Erase heading not required.)

Instructions regarding War Diaries and Intelligence Summaries are contained in F. S. Regs., Part II. and the Staff Manual respectively. Title pages will be prepared in manuscript.

Place	Date	Hour	Summary of Events and Information	Remarks and references to Appendices
ANDAINVILLE	11	9.15am	Orders were received from C.R.A. for the section to proceed to WANEL, also arrived.	
WANEL	12		Ready to meet the Staff Captain to arrange billets. O.C. visited 24 Divisional Train & inspected all animals & arrangements for Contagious Diseases.	
	13		34 Animals were evacuated to No 14 Veterinary Hospital ABBEVILLE. 12 Category "B" men arrived from No 19 Veterinary Hospital in relief of 12 Category "A" men.	
	14		6 Category "A" men were despatched to No 2 Veterinary Hospital. A.D.V.S. XVIII Corps visited the Section in the morning.	
	15		1 Category "A" men despatched. A.D.V.S. XIX Corps visited the Section & informed O.C. that a Veterinary Evacuating Station had been established in the area & that all sick animals could be evacuated to there.	
	16		D.A.D.V.S. 24 Division visited the Section and inspected all animals before being evacuated to V.E.S.	
	17		Section left WANEL for BUIGNY L'ABBÉ. Orders were received to proceed to BEAUVIS WAYENS.	
BUIGNY L'ABBÉ	18			
BEAUVIS WAYENS	19		Moved from BEAUVIS WAYENS to RAMECOURT.	
RAMÉCOURT	20		Arrangements were made with N.C.O. i/c of Veterinary Collecting Post for this	

WAR DIARY
or
INTELLIGENCE SUMMARY.
(Erase heading not required.)

Army Form C. 2118.

Place	Date	Hour	Summary of Events and Information	Remarks and references to Appendices
RAMECOURT	20		Section to evacuate 8 animals through the Collecting Post as this unit was moving at 8 a.m. on 21st inst.	
	21		Section moved from RAMECOURT to LE CAUROY.	
LE CAUROY	22		A.D.V.S. XVIII Corps visited the Section with Staff Captain R.A. who informed O.C. that a Veterinary Evacuating Station had been established at FREVENT.	
	23–29		N.C.O's & Men of this section have been given instruction in the use of the Rifle, and Drill, particularly the 12 Category "B" men who have only joined this unit this month. N.C.O's & Men passed through a Gas Chamber, all Box Respirators were found to be in good order.	
	30			
	30		5 Category "A" men were despatched to No 2 Veterinary Hospital in accordance with D.V.S. Memo No 2/255/18 March 13. 3. 18.	

[signature]
Capt. a V.C.

O.C. 31 Mobile Veterinary Section

Confidential

36 Mobile Veterinary Section

War Diary May 1918.

WAR DIARY or INTELLIGENCE SUMMARY

Army Form C. 2118.

26th MOBILE VETERINARY SECTION
Date May 1918

Place	Date	Hour	Summary of Events and Information	Remarks and references to Appendices
	1			
	2			
	3			
	4		Section left billet at and arrival at billet FOSSE 10, R 2 D 6 3 Sheet 36B, Seynets	
	5		O.C. DADVS advised re location of Section. Detachment from 196 Coy. left & 3 men returned to Section	
	6		27 horses evacuated to CCS BARLIN in afternoon	
	7		Section paraded & went to Divisional Baths	
	8		ADVS corps & DADVS called in evening – inspected sick horses	
	9		22 horses evacuated to CCS BARLIN & another party left billet in aft with 13 horses for CCS BARLIN	
	10		Box respirator drill & practice with helmets on.	
	11		Rifle drill in aft.	
	12			
	13		Box respirator drill in morn 8 horses evacuated to CCS BARLIN in afternoon	
	14			
	15		Section paraded re men promoted to Divisional Baths	
	16		11 Horses evacuated to CCS in morning	

Army Form C. 2118.

WAR DIARY
or
INTELLIGENCE SUMMARY
(Erase heading not required.)

Place	Date	Hour	Summary of Events and Information	Remarks and references to Appendices
In the Field	MAY 17.		14500 Pte HOLMWOOD.J.S. AVC from No 2 VH. retd to duty with 36 MVS	
	18		Nos. 201604. Pte LEE.A. DERBYSHIRE.W (22d Entrenchment Bn) retd to Unit at HQ from temp duty with MVS	
			Nos 17843 26454 14500 26907 28652 411	
			Ptes HAWKES.W, HEWLETT.A, HOLMWOOD.J.S, LEE.A, TWEEDIE.A, STUNT.W.H of 36 MVS transferred to No 18 Vet	
			inary Evacuating Station. Party proceeded by train from BARLIN in afternoon	
	19		15 Horses Evacuated to VES. BARLIN.	
	20		9 " " " " "	
	21		Section paid in afternoon	
	22		Waggon painted 2 men of Section painting waggons	
	23		8 Horses evacuated to 1st Cav VES BARLIN, Waggon painting carried out	
	24		Waggon painting carried out	
	25		" " " "	
	26		13 Horses evacuated to 1st Cav VES BARLIN. Ambulance (horse) painted	
	27		13 Horses evacuated to " " " "	
	28		Waggon painting carried out	
	29		DDVS 1st Army Inspected MVS in afternoon	
	30		" " " "	
	31		12 Horses evacuated to Veterinary Evacuating Station BARLIN.	

Signature
CAPTAIN A.V.C.
O.C. 36 MOBILE VETERINARY SECTION.

Confidential

War Diary

36 Mobile Veterinary Section

For the month of

June 1918.

Army Form C. 2118.

WAR DIARY
or
INTELLIGENCE SUMMARY.
(Erase heading not required.)

Instructions regarding War Diaries and Intelligence Summaries are contained in F. S. Regs., Part II. and the Staff Manual respectively. Title pages will be prepared in manuscript.

Place	Date	Hour	Summary of Events and Information	Remarks and references to Appendices
FOSSE 10	June 1		O.C. inspected all animals of Corpo Troops Divise	
	2		Visited 72nd Infantry Brigade. D.A.D.V.S. examined all animals for evacuation	
	3		Examined animals of 73rd Field Ambulance and Engineer Pool	
	4		D.A.D.V.S. visited the sectors and examined all animals for evacuation	
	5		Inspected animals of D.A.C. section 24th D.A.C. for Corps Divise	
	6		Section busy repairing the places of stable	
	7		Visited 1st Corps Veterinary Evacuating Station also 24th Divisionele Train	
	8		N.C.O.'s now attached Divisional Baths. Examine for sectors in afternoon	
	9		D.A.D.V.S. visited Sectors & examined animals for evacuation	
	10		Visited 72 Infantry Brigade & Section 24th D.A.C. and 73 Field Ambulance	
	11		Inspected animals of 96 Heavy Labour Coy and Engineer Pool	
	12		Examined all animals of 24th Divisionele Train for Corps Divise	
	13		Section busy making harness & boot dressing & making of billets	
	14		14 Surgical Cases evacuated to 1st Corps V.E.S.	
	15			

Army Form C. 2118.

WAR DIARY
or
INTELLIGENCE SUMMARY.
(Erase heading not required.)

Instructions regarding War Diaries and Intelligence Summaries are contained in F. S. Regs., Part II. and the Staff Manual respectively. Title pages will be prepared in manuscript.

Place	Date	Hour	Summary of Events and Information	Remarks and references to Appendices
FOSSE 10	16		Visited units of 72 Infantry Brigade, also S.A.A. section 24th D.A.C.	
	17		Inspected animals of 73 Field Ambulance and 24th Divisional Train	
	18		D.A.D.V.S. visits to billets are ceasing. All animals for evacuation	
	19		One case of suspected Mange admitted, treated and returned to unit for duty.	
	20-24th		Two ponies I have slipped with hind quarters received for trial, and to be improved on by 24th inst. To hipper were found not to be a decided improvement, but the hind have not fallen off. 40 ponies sent the front on	
	25		Visited S.A.A. section 24th D.A.C. 5 doubtful cases evacuated to 1st Corps V.F.S.	
	26		O.C. took over temporary duties of D.A. D.V.S. 24th Division during the temporary absence of the D.A.D.V.S. on leave to ENGLAND.	
	27		Visited 24th Divisional Train and 72 Infantry Brigade.	
	28		Visited offices of D.A.D.V.S. and examined animals of #73 Field Ambulance.	
	29		One case of suspected Mange admitted from 110 Hy. Bty. R.G.A. A.D.V.S. XVIII Corps called on the evening and discussed the animal. This case was treated with	
	30		Calomel Sulphide and returned to unit for duty. One case of Mange admitted from 126 A.T.R.B. Microscope gave positive diagnosis. The animal was evacuated	

O.C. 36 Mobile Veterinary Section

J.R. Currie Capt. A.V.C.

Confidential

War Diary

36 Mobile Veterinary Section

For the month of

July 1918

Army Form C. 2118.

WAR DIARY
or
INTELLIGENCE SUMMARY.
(Erase heading not required.)

Instructions regarding War Diaries and Intelligence Summaries are contained in F. S. Regs., Part II. and the Staff Manual respectively. Title pages will be prepared in manuscript.

Place	Date	Hour	Summary of Events and Information	Remarks and references to Appendices
FOSSE 10	JULY 1		Visited 73rd Field Ambulance and inspected all their animals for Contagious Disease.	
	2		Attended office of D.A.D.V.S. 24th Division and inspected animals of 24th Signal Coy.	
	3		Visited 24th Divisional Train and examined all animals for Contagious Disease.	
	4		Meeting of Division transport Officers reports.	
	5		Attended office of D.A.D.V.S. and interviewed Veterinary Officers of the Division.	
	6		Inspected animals of 72nd Infantry Brigade.	
	7		Visited 1.a.a. Section 24th D.A.C. and examined all animals for Contagious Disease.	
	8		Examined scrapings of 3 animals belonging to 126 A.F.A.B. for Mange. Result Negative.	
	9		N.C.O's + Men passed in full marching order. No deficiencies in kit were found.	
	10		Examined scrapings of 3 animals from 8"C.A.F.A.B. for Mange. 2 Positive, 1 Negative.	
	11		D.A.D.V.S. returned from leave. Visited 73rd Field Ambulance	
	12		Attended office of D.A.D.V.S. + reported to him all matters pertinent that occurred during his absence on leave in ENGLAND.	
	13		D.A.D.V.S. visited Division and examined all animals for evacuation.	
	14		Action drew 6 loads of Broadcast from Cuinchy Forestry to furnish enclosures.	
	15		Inspected all animals of 24th Divisional Train for Contagious Disease.	

Army Form C. 2118.

WAR DIARY
or
INTELLIGENCE SUMMARY.
(Erase heading not required.)

Instructions regarding War Diaries and Intelligence Summaries are contained in F. S. Regs., Part II. and the Staff Manual respectively. Title pages will be prepared in manuscript.

Place	Date	Hour	Summary of Events and Information	Remarks and references to Appendices
FOSSE 10	July 16		D.A.D.V.S. visited the section and examined all animals prior to evacuation.	
	17		All animals of S.A.A. section 24th B.A.C. examined for Contagious Disease.	
	18		Scabious Horses taken from Annual of 126 A. F. A. B. unit Positive	
	19–25		Section preparing billet to the winter, bathroom and Pharmacy erected. Icehouse utensils and thermometers up with shelves etc.	
	26		Sick case of Lymphangitis Mange from 126 A F A B admitted. Scabious microscopically. Parasites were found over the animals examined.	
	27		Animals of 72nd Infantry Brigade examined for Contagious diseases.	
	28		Examined Remounts for Contagious disease at No 1 Coy. 34th Divisional Train.	
	29			
	31		No 505.1 Ste Wright. J. A. V. C. proceeds with Motorious strain Mule ridden by VIII 16 Corps Commander. O.C. no 14 M.V.S. 11th Division arranges the loan of this ambulance.	
	31		Three cases of Lymphangitis Mange evacuated from 126 A. F. A. B. to No 1 V.E.S.	

X. W. Maurer Capt A.V.C.
OC 36 Mobile Veterinary Section

Confidential

War Diary

36 Mobile Veterinary Section

For the month of

August 1918.

Army Form C. 2118.

WAR DIARY
or
INTELLIGENCE SUMMARY.
(Erase heading not required.)

Place	Date	Hour	Summary of Events and Information	Remarks and references to Appendices
FOSSE 10	AUGUST 1		Visited 24th Divisional Train and inspected all animals for Contagious Diseases	
	2		D.A.D.V.S. visited the Audits and inspected all animals prior to evacuation	
	3		Visited 72 Infantry Brigade and 73 Field Ambulance	
	4		Audits reopening both mornings. D.A.D.V.S. visited the sections	
	5		Capt W.R. Maginnis A.V.C. taken over the duties during the absence of Capt J H Lamy A.V.C. on leave	
	6		D.A.D.V.S. inspected all our animals previous to evacuation	
	7		O.C. visited 24th Divisional Train 1 A.C. Divison 24th D.A.C & 73 Field Ambulance	
	8		A.A & Q.M.G. 2nd Division visited the sections inspected Catahouse site	
	9		Catahouse pulled down & rebuilt. Mess room rebuilt. Grease Traps put up	
	10		D.A.D.V.S. inspected Catahouse, Billets, Pharmacy, Stables etc & drainage	
	11		Notification received that VIII Corps Commander would inspect Section on 13 inst	
	12		9 Cases of Barbed Wounds admitted from 52 ADAB and 3 from 1st N. Staff Rifle	
	13		Corps Commander inspected Section Stables, Pharmacy, Saddlerooms & Forage Barn	
	14		Section Billets shelled in afternoon all horses taken to AIX NOULETTE.	
	15		O.C. visited BOYEFFLES, SAINS EN GOHELLE for billets	

WAR DIARY
or
INTELLIGENCE SUMMARY.

Army Form C. 2118.

Place	Date	Hour	Summary of Events and Information	Remarks and references to Appendices
FOSSE 10	16		Section moved from FOSSE 10 to BOUVIGNY-BOYEFFLES.	
BOUVIGNY-BOYEFFLES	17 to 20		N.C.O's + Men fixing up horse standings, 2 men left at FOSSE 10 to pull down all material for building stables. Horse count returned to No 1 V.E.S. BARLIN.	
	21		Capt J. H. Lorne A.V.C. returned from leave. Capt W. A. May of A.V.C. returned to his See 24 D.A.C.	
	22-31		During this period G.S. Wagon + Maltese carts have been drawing Rd Metal, Sand &c. for floors of horse standings. A cook place has been erected. Cookhouse & Men's Room built. Drainage system has been completed. Forge Barn fixed up. G.O.C. 24 Division + A.A. & Q.M.G. 24 Division have inspected the billets, which is being prepared for winter quarters. N.C.O's and men have been inoculated at the rate of our per day. The cases of Barbed Wounds were received from S.B.A. T.M.B. and 16th Inov. while were incurred to No 1 V.E.S., A.A. & Q.M.G. and A.D.M.S. 24 Division inspected Cookhouse etc.	

J. H. Lorne Capt A.V.C.
O.C. 36 Mobile Veterinary Section

Confidential

War Diary

36 Mobile Veterinary Section

For the month

of

September 1918.

Army Form C. 2118.

WAR DIARY
or
INTELLIGENCE SUMMARY.
(Erase heading not required.)

Instructions regarding War Diaries and Intelligence Summaries are contained in F.S. Regs., Part II. and the Staff Manual respectively. Title pages will be prepared in manuscript.

Place	Date	Hour	Summary of Events and Information	Remarks and references to Appendices
BOUVIGNY	Sept 1/1916		D.A.D.V.S. 24th Division visited the sick row & examined animals for evacuation	
	2		It Visited 24th Divisional Train and examined animals for Contagious Disease	
	3		Visited 24th D.A.C. and 1st Royal Fusiliers	
	4		Sick row on fatigues preparing billet for the winter season	
	5		D.A.D.V.S. 24th Division visited the sick row & examined a case of Mange	
	6		from M.M.P. 24th Division. Animal treated and returned to unit.	
	7		Visited 24th Divisional Train & 24th D.A.C.	
	8		A.D.V.S. VIII Corps inspected Sick row Billet.	
	9		A.A. & Q.M.G. 24th Division inspected Sick row Billet.	
	10		Visited No 1 & 2 Sections 24th D.A.C.	
	11		Visited D.A.D.V.S. at SAINS EN GOHELLE & A.A. Section 24th D.A.C.	
	12		D.A.D.V.S. examined animals for evacuation, 2 mm Inoculation at 10 a.m.	
	13		Sick row on fatigues erecting a sick room & ablution bench.	
	14		Visited 24th Divisional Train.	

Army Form. C. 2118.

WAR DIARY
or
INTELLIGENCE SUMMARY.
(Erase heading not required.)

Instructions regarding War Diaries and Intelligence Summaries are contained in F. S. Regs., Part II. and the Staff Manual respectively. Title pages will be prepared in manuscript.

Place	Date	Hour	Summary of Events and Information	Remarks and references to Appendices
BOUVIGNY	15-23		Section on fatigues, finishing off the billets for winter quarters.	
	24		D.A.D.V.S. visited Section	
	25		A.D.V.S. Corps visited & inspected Section & billet. AA & QMG VIII Corps inspected the billet	
	26-27		Section on fatigues erecting a Dressing Ward. D.A.D.V.S. visited the Section & orders received to move on morning of 30, with 2x Divisional Train.	
	28			
	29		Section loading vehicles ready for line of March.	
	30		Section left BOUVIGNY-BOYEFFLES at 3.10 p.m. & arrived at ETREE-WAMIN at 7.15 a.m. and orders received to proceed to LUCHEUL on morning of 1st prox.	

A. W. [signature]
Capt. A.V.C.
O.C. 36 Mobile Veterinary Section

Confidential

War Diary

36 Mobile Veterinary Section

For the month of October 1918.

Army Form C. 2118.

WAR DIARY
or
INTELLIGENCE SUMMARY.
(Erase heading not required.)

Instructions regarding War Diaries and Intelligence Summaries are contained in F. S. Regs., Part II. and the Staff Manual respectively. Title pages will be prepared in manuscript.

Place	Date	Hour	Summary of Events and Information	Remarks and references to Appendices
LA FOLIE FARM. L'ECHEUR.	Oct. 1		Section busy cleaning up billets (Rest Area)	
	2		Saddlery cleaned up ready for billing of horses. D.A.D.V.S visited the section	
	3		Visited at divisional train and inspected all animals for contagious diseases	
	4		Section preparing for line of march. D.A.D.V.S visited the section	
	5		Section moved from LA FOLIE FARM to MERCATEL	
MERCATEL	6		Section left MERCATEL and arrived at MOEUVRES	
MOEUVRES	7		General fatigues etc. OC visited units of the Division. D.A.D.V.S. called	
	8		N.C.O and 2 men sent out to an Advanced Post to take over wounded animals.	
	9	2pm	Section left MOEUVRES and arrived at GRAINCOURT at 4p.m	
GRAINCOURT	10	8am	Section left GRAINCOURT for RUMILLY. At 5p.m section left RUMILLY for CAURIOR	
CAURIOR.	11		Wounded Animals from various units were admitted to this section & treated.	
	12		33 Wounded Animals evacuated to VI Corps V.E.S & XVII Corps V.E.S had not moved up to MARCOING.	
	13	2pm	Section left CAURIOR for AYESNES-LES-AUBERT	
AYESNES-LES-AUBERT.	14		D.A.D.V.S. visited section & inspected billets. O.C visited units of the Division	

Army Form C. 2118.

WAR DIARY
or
INTELLIGENCE SUMMARY.
(Erase heading not required.)

Instructions regarding War Diaries and Intelligence Summaries are contained in F. S. Regs., Part II. and the Staff Manual respectively. Title pages will be prepared in manuscript.

Place	Date	Hour	Summary of Events and Information	Remarks and references to Appendices
AVESNES-LES-AUBERT	15		27 Wounded animals evacuated to XVII Corps V.E.S. at MARCOING	
	16		O.C. visited 24 Divisional Train 72nd Infantry Brigade & 24th Machine Gun Bn.	
	17		Section preparing to move to Rest Area	
	18	8.30 am	Section left AVESNES-LES-AUBERT for CAMBRAI. 14 animals evacuated to XVII Corps	
			V.E.S. whilst on the line of March. XVII Corps V.E.S. now at CAMBRAI.	
CAMBRAI	19		Section cleaning up billet & appurtenances. D.A.D.V.S. visited the Section.	
	20-25		Veterinary animals admitted to the Section during this period coming to the Division (Corps	
			Artillery) being on "Rest". O.C. visited units of the Division A.D.V.S XVII Corps	
			visited the Section and inspected the billet.	
	26	11 am	Section left CAMBRAI for ST AUBERT. Attachment joined 73rd Infantry Brigade	
ST AUBERT	27		General tidying & cleaning up billet etc. D.A.D.V.S. visited the Section.	
	28		O.C. visited 24 Divisional Train 72nd Infantry Brigade, 3 Field Co. R.E.	
	29		O.C. visited 24 D.A.C. D.A.D.V.S. inspected animals previous to evacuation.	
	30		1 case of Gas Poisoning admitted to Section from 106 Bde R.F.A. and transit	

J. L. [signature]
Capt A.V.C.
O.C. 36 Mobile Veterinary Section

Army Form C. 2118
36 M.U. Very see
Vol 4 0

WAR DIARY
or
INTELLIGENCE SUMMARY.
(Erase heading not required.)

Instructions regarding War Diaries and Intelligence Summaries are contained in F.S. Regs., Part II. and the Staff Manual respectively. Title pages will be prepared in manuscript.

Place	Date	Hour	Summary of Events and Information	Remarks and references to Appendices
NOVEMBER	11	12-30.	Armistice terms signed by the Enemy. Remainder of month we have been busy sitting in a rear area with a view to obtaining much demobilisation. Sorting, mending and renewing Kit and a entrainment of Mules.	

W. Cox Captain O/C
O.C. 36 M/U Ypres, Ledgers.

T.2134. Wt. W708-776. 500000. 4/15. Sir J.C. & S.

On His Majesty's Service.

The O.i.C.
G.H.Q.
3rd Echelon
British E.F.

Army Form C. 2118

WAR DIARY
or
INTELLIGENCE SUMMARY

36 Mob Vety Sec

(Erase heading not required.)

Vol 4.1

Place	Date	Hour	Summary of Events and Information	Remarks and references to Appendices
LANDAS	DEC 19		Section left LANDAS for TOURNAI.	
TOURNAI	24		D.D.V.S. First Army and A.D.V.S. I Corps visited the Section	
	25		D.D.V.S. Fifth Army visited the Section.	
	27		D.V.S. & D.D.V.S. Fifth Army inspected the Section billets.	

Mal. Trappa Capt. R.A.V.C.
O.C. 36 Mobile Veterinary Section

16/3 24
36 Mot Vety Sec
Army Form C. 2118

WAR DIARY
or
INTELLIGENCE SUMMARY
(Erase heading not required.)

Place	Date	Hour	Summary of Events and Information	Remarks and references to Appendices
LA TOMBE	Jan 1919 24		During this month all animals of 24th Division have been classified for Demobilization purposes. D.D.V.S Field Army and A.D.V.S. I Corps inspected and Cast all Class "D" animals. 132 for sale to civilians and 37 for sale to Butcher.	WSL 42
	27		All animals for sale to civilians were tested on the Aultron with Mallein and returned to their units.	

Wgwacmp
Capt R.A.V.C.
O.C. 36 Mobile Veterinary Section

WAR DIARY or INTELLIGENCE SUMMARY

Army Form C. 2118

36 Mot Veterinary Section

Vol 4 3

Place	Date	Hour	Summary of Events and Information	Remarks and references to Appendices
LA TOMBE	Feby 1-23		During this period all animals of Classes A.Y. B.Y. C.Z, A.X & B.X. have been treated with Mallein. All animals of Class C.Z. have been inspected & Branded with the letter "Z" on the NS quarter	
	19th		A.D.V.S. I Corps inspected 100 Class C.Z animals	
TOURNAI	24		Section left # LA TOMBE and moved to RUE DE LANNOY, TOURNAI. 100 animals sold by Public Auction at TOURNAI.	
	25			
	27		A.D.V.S. I Corps inspected 150 animals Class Z, these were however ready for sale by Public Auction on 4th prox.	

W Arrington Capt R.A.V.C.
O.C. 36 Mobile Veterinary Section

Army Form C. 2118.

WAR DIARY
or
INTELLIGENCE SUMMARY.
(Erase heading not required.)

Instructions regarding War Diaries and Intelligence Summaries are contained in F. S. Regs., Part II. and the Staff Manual respectively. Title pages will be prepared in manuscript.

Place	Date	Hour	Summary of Events and Information	Remarks and references to Appendices
TOURNAI	March 5	10.30	Mare evacuated S.Thomas to NOIVES	
		7	Horses evacuated to NOIVES	
	12		Captain Barker's rank with war temporary command of 36 MVS whilst OC 36 MVS	
			Capt. MacGregor A. was to ENGLAND on leave	
	17	5	Horses evacuated to NOIVES	
	18	13	Horses evacuated Poilus to LDS late 13 proceeded to HAVRE BX for ENGLAND	
		13.	Mules cast as TOURNAI OC MVS in charge of all animals cast	
		31	Mules cast " " turned to Cretans handed over to 24th Divisional Train	
TOURNAI	9/4/19	7	4 mar transferred to No 6 Mob. Vet. Sec. Fried Deer	

W. Murray, CAPTAIN A.V.C.
O.C. 36 MOBILE VETERINARY SECTION.

[Stamp: 36th MOBILE VETERINARY SECTION 9/4/19]

www.ingramcontent.com/pod-product-compliance
Lightning Source LLC
Chambersburg PA
CBHW081425160426
43193CB00013B/2199